Mastering Python OOP: A Beginner's Guide to Object-Oriented Programming

Anshuman Mishra

Published by Anshuman Mishra, 2025.

"MASTERING PYTHON OOP: A BEGINNER'S GUIDE TO OBJECT-ORIENTED PROGRAMMING"

TABLE OF CONTENTS

ABOUT THE BOOK:

"MASTERING PYTHON OOP: A BEGINNER'S GUIDE TO OBJECT-ORIENTED PROGRAMMING"

OBJECT-ORIENTED PROGRAMMING (OOP) IS A FUNDAMENTAL CONCEPT IN MODERN SOFTWARE DEVELOPMENT, AND PYTHON IS ONE OF THE MOST POPULAR PROGRAMMING LANGUAGES TO LEARN IT. THIS BOOK, DESIGNED FOR ABSOLUTE BEGINNERS, FOCUSES EXCLUSIVELY ON UNDERSTANDING OOP PRINCIPLES AND APPLYING THEM EFFECTIVELY USING PYTHON.

WHETHER YOU'RE A STUDENT, A BUDDING PROGRAMMER, OR SOMEONE SWITCHING TO PROGRAMMING FROM ANOTHER FIELD, **"MASTERING PYTHON OOP"** PROVIDES A CLEAR, STEP-BY-STEP INTRODUCTION TO THE CORE CONCEPTS OF OBJECT-ORIENTED PROGRAMMING, MAKING IT EASY FOR YOU TO WRITE EFFICIENT AND REUSABLE CODE.

WHAT THIS BOOK OFFERS:

1. **BEGINNER-FRIENDLY APPROACH**
   - NO PRIOR PROGRAMMING EXPERIENCE IS REQUIRED. THE BOOK STARTS WITH THE BASICS AND GRADUALLY BUILDS UP TO ADVANCED OOP CONCEPTS IN PYTHON.

2. **HANDS-ON LEARNING**
   - EACH CHAPTER INCLUDES PRACTICAL EXAMPLES, CODING EXERCISES, AND PROJECTS THAT HELP SOLIDIFY YOUR UNDERSTANDING OF OOP CONCEPTS.

3. **COMPREHENSIVE COVERAGE**
   - FROM CLASSES, OBJECTS, AND INHERITANCE TO ADVANCED TOPICS LIKE ABSTRACTION AND OPERATOR OVERLOADING, THIS BOOK COVERS EVERYTHING YOU NEED TO KNOW TO MASTER OOP IN PYTHON.

4. **CLEAR EXPLANATIONS**
   - EVERY CONCEPT IS EXPLAINED IN SIMPLE LANGUAGE, WITH STEP-BY-STEP INSTRUCTIONS AND VISUAL AIDS WHERE NEEDED.

KEY FEATURES OF THE BOOK:

- **FOCUSED SYLLABUS:** EXCLUSIVELY OOP CONCEPTS, TAILORED FOR BEGINNERS IN PYTHON.
- **PRACTICAL EXAMPLES:** REAL-WORLD SCENARIOS TO MAKE LEARNING ENGAGING AND RELATABLE.
- **ERROR HANDLING:** TIPS AND TECHNIQUES TO DEBUG AND MANAGE EXCEPTIONS.
- **INTERVIEW PREPARATION:** COMMON PYTHON OOP QUESTIONS AND ANSWERS INCLUDED AS A BONUS.
- **ADVANCED INSIGHTS:** OPTIONAL ADVANCED TOPICS LIKE METACLASSES AND DESIGN PATTERNS FOR THOSE WHO WANT TO EXPLORE FURTHER.

WHO SHOULD READ THIS BOOK?

- **STUDENTS** WHO WANT A BEGINNER-FRIENDLY INTRODUCTION TO PYTHON AND OOP.
- **EDUCATORS** LOOKING FOR A RESOURCE TO TEACH PYTHON OOP EFFECTIVELY.
- **CAREER CHANGERS** OR ASPIRING DEVELOPERS LEARNING PYTHON FOR CAREER GROWTH.
- **PROGRAMMING ENTHUSIASTS** CURIOUS ABOUT MASTERING OBJECT-ORIENTED PROGRAMMING.

BY THE END OF THIS BOOK, READERS WILL HAVE A SOLID FOUNDATION IN PYTHON OOP AND THE CONFIDENCE TO WRITE CLEAN, EFFICIENT, AND REUSABLE CODE FOR PERSONAL OR PROFESSIONAL PROJECTS.

ABOUT THE AUTHOR

ANSHUMAN MISHRA, AN ACCOMPLISHED ACADEMIC AND EDUCATOR, HAS OVER 18 YEARS OF TEACHING EXPERIENCE AS AN ASSISTANT PROFESSOR IN COMPUTER SCIENCE. HE HOLDS AN M.TECH IN COMPUTER SCIENCE FROM THE PRESTIGIOUS BIRLA INSTITUTE OF TECHNOLOGY, MESRA. CURRENTLY SERVING AT DORANDA COLLEGE, RANCHI, HE SPECIALIZES IN PROGRAMMING LANGUAGES, SOFTWARE DEVELOPMENT, AND COMPUTER SKILLS, INSPIRING COUNTLESS STUDENTS WITH HIS PROFOUND KNOWLEDGE AND PRACTICAL INSIGHTS.

ANSHUMAN IS A PASSIONATE WRITER WITH EXPERTISE IN CREATING EDUCATIONAL RESOURCES FOR STUDENTS AND PROFESSIONALS. HIS BOOKS COVER TOPICS LIKE JAVA PROGRAMMING, SQL, OPERATING SYSTEMS, AND COMPETITIVE PROGRAMMING, REFLECTING HIS DEDICATION TO MAKING COMPLEX SUBJECTS ACCESSIBLE AND ENGAGING.

BEYOND ACADEMICS, ANSHUMAN IS A MOTIVATIONAL THINKER, A LOVER OF MYSTERIES, AND A STORYTELLER AT HEART. HE HAS AUTHORED WORKS RANGING FROM SELF-MOTIVATION GUIDES TO CHILDREN'S STORIES AND BOOKS DELVING INTO THE RICH HISTORY AND CULTURE OF JHARKHAND. HIS ABILITY TO WEAVE KNOWLEDGE WITH INSPIRATION MAKES HIS BOOKS A TREASURE FOR READERS OF ALL AGES.

"Programs must be written for people to read, and only incidentally for machines to execute."
— Harold Abelson & Gerald Jay Sussman, *Structure and Interpretation of Computer Programs*

Copyright Page

Title: **MASTERING PYTHON OOP: A BEGINNER'S GUIDE TO OBJECT-ORIENTED PROGRAMMING**

CHAPTER 1: INTRODUCTION TO OBJECT-ORIENTED PROGRAMMING (OOP)

1. Introduction to OOP in Python

This section lays the groundwork for understanding OOP and why Python is an ideal language for beginners. It includes:

- **What is Object-Oriented Programming?**
  A clear explanation of OOP principles: encapsulation, inheritance, polymorphism, and abstraction.
  Example:

```
class Person:
    def __init__(self, name, age):
        self.name = name
        self.age = age

    def introduce(self):
        return f"My name is {self.name}, and I am {self.age}
years old."

p1 = Person("Alice", 25)
print(p1.introduce())
```

  Here, `Person` is a class, and `p1` is an object. The method `introduce` demonstrates encapsulation by keeping the implementation details within the class.

Classes and objects are the foundational elements of Object-Oriented Programming (OOP). A class is a blueprint for creating objects, which are instances of the class. Objects combine data (attributes) and behavior (methods), encapsulating them within a single entity.

---

2. Defining Classes and Creating Objects

1. Defining a Class

A class is defined using the `class` keyword, and it contains attributes and methods. Attributes store data, and methods define behaviors or functionalities.

2. The `__init__` Method

The __init__ method is a special method in Python, also called the constructor. It is automatically invoked when an object is created from a class. It initializes the object's attributes.

3. Creating Objects

Objects are created by calling the class name as if it were a function. The arguments passed are used to initialize the object.

Example:

```
class Car:
    # Constructor to initialize brand and model
    def __init__(self, brand, model):
        self.brand = brand  # Instance variable
        self.model = model  # Instance variable

    # Method to display car information
    def display_info(self):
        return f"Car: {self.brand} {self.model}"

# Creating an object of the Car class
my_car = Car("Toyota", "Corolla")

# Accessing the method of the object
print(my_car.display_info())  # Output: Car: Toyota Corolla
```

- **Explanation:**
    - `Car` is a class with attributes `brand` and `model`, and a method `display_info`.
    - `my_car` is an object (or instance) of the `Car` class.
    - `display_info` is called on the object to retrieve the car's details.

Instance vs. Class Variables

Variables in a class can either be:

1. **Instance Variables:** Unique to each object, accessed using `self`.
2. **Class Variables:** Shared across all objects of the class, accessed using the class name.

Example:

```
class Car:
    # Class variable
```

```
        wheels = 4

        def __init__(self, brand, model):
            self.brand = brand   # Instance variable
            self.model = model   # Instance variable

        def display_info(self):
            return f"Car: {self.brand} {self.model}, Wheels: {Car.wheels}"
# Creating objects
car1 = Car("Toyota", "Corolla")
car2 = Car("Honda", "Civic")

# Accessing instance and class variables
print(car1.display_info())   # Output: Car: Toyota Corolla, Wheels: 4
print(car2.display_info())   # Output: Car: Honda Civic, Wheels: 4

# Modifying class variable
Car.wheels = 6
print(car1.display_info())   # Output: Car: Toyota Corolla, Wheels: 6
print(car2.display_info())   # Output: Car: Honda Civic, Wheels: 6

# Modifying instance variable
car1.brand = "Ford"
print(car1.display_info())   # Output: Car: Ford Corolla, Wheels: 6
```

- **Instance Variables:**
  - Defined within methods using `self`.
  - Unique to each object (e.g., `brand` and `model`).
  - Changes affect only the specific object.
- **Class Variables:**
  - Defined directly within the class body.
  - Shared among all objects (e.g., `wheels`).
  - Changes affect all objects of the class.

Key Points:

- Use instance variables for data specific to individual objects.
- Use class variables for data shared across all instances of the class.
- The `self` keyword in Python refers to the instance on which a method is called and is used to access instance variables.

---

3. Encapsulation

Encapsulation is one of the core principles of Object-Oriented Programming (OOP). It involves bundling data (attributes) and methods (functions) that operate on the data into a single entity, such as a class, and restricting direct access to some of the object's components. This ensures controlled access to the internal state of an object and prevents accidental interference or misuse.

Private and Public Attributes

Python provides access control through naming conventions:

1. **Public Attributes:** These are accessible from anywhere and are defined without any special prefix.
2. **Protected Attributes:** These are indicated with a single underscore (_) and suggest that they should only be accessed within the class or its subclasses.
3. **Private Attributes:** These are indicated with a double underscore (__) and are not directly accessible outside the class.

Example: Private Attributes

```
class BankAccount:
    def __init__(self, balance):
        self.__balance = balance  # Private attribute

    def get_balance(self):
        """Public method to access the private attribute."""
        return self.__balance

    def deposit(self, amount):
        """Public method to modify the private attribute."""
        if amount > 0:
            self.__balance += amount
        else:
            print("Deposit amount must be positive.")

# Creating an object of BankAccount
account = BankAccount(1000)

# Modifying and accessing balance using methods
account.deposit(500)
print(account.get_balance())  # Outputs: 1500

# Attempting direct access to the private attribute
# print(account.__balance)  # Raises AttributeError
```

- **Explanation:**
    - The __balance attribute is private and cannot be accessed directly.
    - Public methods get_balance and deposit are provided to interact with the __balance attribute.
    - Encapsulation ensures that the balance attribute is accessed or modified only through the defined methods, maintaining data integrity.

Using Getter and Setter Methods

Getter and setter methods allow controlled access to private attributes. Getters retrieve the value of an attribute, while setters update its value after validation or additional logic.

Example: Getter and Setter

```
class BankAccount:
    def __init__(self, balance):
        self.__balance = balance  # Private attribute

    def get_balance(self):
        """Getter method to access the balance."""
        return self.__balance

    def set_balance(self, new_balance):
        """Setter method to modify the balance with validation."""
        if new_balance >= 0:
            self.__balance = new_balance
        else:
            print("Balance cannot be negative.")

# Creating an object of BankAccount
account = BankAccount(1000)

# Using getter to retrieve the balance
print(account.get_balance())  # Outputs: 1000

# Using setter to modify the balance
account.set_balance(2000)
print(account.get_balance())  # Outputs: 2000

# Invalid modification using setter
account.set_balance(-500)  # Outputs: Balance cannot be negative.
```

- **Explanation:**
    - The `get_balance` method retrieves the value of `__balance`.
    - The `set_balance` method updates the value of `__balance` after checking if the new balance is non-negative.
    - This ensures that the attribute is updated only with valid data.

Key Points of Encapsulation

1. **Data Protection:** Private attributes ensure sensitive data is protected from unintended external modifications.
2. **Controlled Access:** Public methods (getters and setters) provide a controlled way to access or modify private attributes.
3. **Code Flexibility:** Logic for accessing or modifying data can be changed within the methods without affecting the external code that uses the class.

Real-World Analogy

Encapsulation is like a bank's ATM. The money (data) is stored securely inside the machine (private attribute). Customers (external entities) interact with the ATM using the keypad and screen (public methods), ensuring that the money is handled in a controlled and secure way.

This principle in Python makes your code more robust, secure, and easier to maintain.

4. Inheritance

- **Single and Multiple Inheritance**
  Demonstrates how to reuse code by inheriting attributes and methods from a parent class.

```
class Animal:
    def speak(self):
        return "I make a sound."

class Dog(Animal):
    def speak(self):
        return "Woof!"

d = Dog()
print(d.speak())   # Outputs: Woof!
```

- **Using `super()` for Method Overriding**
  Explains how `super()` allows access to parent class methods.

5. Polymorphism

- **Method Overriding**
  Demonstrates how derived classes can have methods with the same name but different behavior.
- **Practical Example of Polymorphism**

```
class Shape:
    def area(self):
        pass

class Rectangle(Shape):
    def area(self, length, width):
        return length * width

class Circle(Shape):
    def area(self, radius):
        return 3.14 * radius * radius

shapes = [Rectangle(), Circle()]
print(shapes[0].area(5, 3))   # Outputs: 15
print(shapes[1].area(7))      # Outputs: 153.86
```

6. Abstraction

Abstraction is one of the fundamental principles of Object-Oriented Programming (OOP). It focuses on hiding the internal details of how something works and exposing only the essential functionality. In Python, abstraction can be achieved using **abstract classes** and **abstract methods**.

Abstract Classes and Methods

An **abstract class** is a blueprint for other classes. It cannot be instantiated directly and is used to define methods that must be implemented in any subclass. Python provides the abc (Abstract Base Classes) module to create abstract classes and methods.

- **Abstract Method:** A method declared in the abstract class but has no implementation in it. It must be implemented in derived classes.

Using the abc Module

The abc module provides the tools to create abstract classes and methods using the @abstractmethod decorator.

Example: Abstract Class and Abstract Method

```
from abc import ABC, abstractmethod

# Abstract class
```

```
class Vehicle(ABC):
    @abstractmethod
    def start_engine(self):
        """Abstract method that must be implemented in derived
classes."""
        pass

# Concrete class inheriting the abstract class
class Car(Vehicle):
    def start_engine(self):
        """Concrete implementation of the abstract method."""
        print("Engine started.")

# Instantiating a concrete class
c = Car()
c.start_engine()  # Outputs: Engine started.
```

Explanation of the Code

1. **Abstract Class (`Vehicle`):**
   - Defined as a subclass of `ABC`.
   - Contains an abstract method `start_engine` decorated with `@abstractmethod`.
2. **Concrete Class (`Car`):**
   - Inherits the abstract class `Vehicle`.
   - Implements the abstract method `start_engine`.
3. **Key Features:**
   - If the `Car` class does not implement the `start_engine` method, Python will raise a `TypeError` when you try to create an object of `Car`.
   - The `Vehicle` class serves as a blueprint, enforcing a specific structure for its derived classes.

Why Use Abstract Classes and Methods?

- **Enforce Implementation:** Ensure that all derived classes implement the required methods.
- **Design Consistency:** Helps maintain a consistent interface across all derived classes.
- **Prevent Instantiation:** Prevents instantiation of incomplete or base classes.

Real-World Analogy

Think of an abstract class as a contract. For example:

- **Abstract Class (Blueprint):** A "Vehicle" that declares the common functionality `start_engine`.
- **Concrete Implementations:** Specific types of vehicles like `Car`, `Bike`, or `Truck`, each with its unique way of starting the engine.

This ensures that all derived classes adhere to the blueprint while providing their specific implementations.

Additional Example with Multiple Abstract Methods

```python
from abc import ABC, abstractmethod

# Abstract class
class Animal(ABC):
    @abstractmethod
    def speak(self):
        pass

    @abstractmethod
    def move(self):
        pass

# Concrete class implementing both abstract methods
class Dog(Animal):
    def speak(self):
        return "Woof!"

    def move(self):
        return "The dog runs."

# Concrete class implementing both abstract methods
class Bird(Animal):
    def speak(self):
        return "Chirp!"

    def move(self):
        return "The bird flies."

# Instantiating concrete classes
dog = Dog()
bird = Bird()

print(dog.speak())    # Outputs: Woof!
print(dog.move())     # Outputs: The dog runs.
```

```
print(bird.speak()) # Outputs: Chirp!
print(bird.move())  # Outputs: The bird flies.
```

Benefits of Abstraction

1. **Flexibility:** Allows changes in the underlying implementation without altering the exposed interface.
2. **Security:** Hides unnecessary details from the user, reducing complexity.
3. **Extensibility:** Makes it easy to extend and maintain the code as new requirements arise.

Key Takeaways

- Abstract classes define the structure and behavior that derived classes must follow.
- Abstract methods ensure that specific functionality is implemented in all derived classes.
- The `abc` module and `@abstractmethod` decorator are powerful tools for implementing abstraction in Python.

7. Special Methods and Operator Overloading

- **Customizing Class Behavior**
  Shows how to override special methods like `__str__`, `__repr__`, and arithmetic operators.

```
class Point:
    def __init__(self, x, y):
        self.x = x
        self.y = y

    def __add__(self, other):
        return Point(self.x + other.x, self.y + other.y)

    def __str__(self):
        return f"Point({self.x}, {self.y})"

p1 = Point(1, 2)
p2 = Point(3, 4)
print(p1 + p2)  # Outputs: Point(4, 6)
```

MCQ

1. Which of the following best defines Object-Oriented Programming?

- (a) Programming with procedures.
- (b) Programming with objects and classes.
- (c) Programming with data structures.
- (d) Programming with functional paradigms.
  Answer: (b)
  Explanation: OOP is a programming paradigm based on the concept of objects and classes that encapsulate data and behavior.

2. What does the term "class" represent in OOP?

- (a) An instance of an object.
- (b) A blueprint for creating objects.
- (c) A function definition.
- (d) A data type.
  Answer: (b)
  Explanation: A class is a blueprint or template that defines the properties and methods for the objects.

3. What is the primary purpose of OOP?

- (a) To perform calculations faster.
- (b) To simplify code reuse and modularity.
- (c) To focus solely on data.
- (d) To avoid using functions.
  Answer: (b)
  Explanation: OOP simplifies code reuse through inheritance and modularity by breaking the code into objects.

4. Which of the following is not a feature of OOP?

- (a) Encapsulation.
- (b) Polymorphism.
- (c) Procedural execution.

- (d) Inheritance.

Answer: (c)

Explanation: Procedural execution is a feature of procedural programming, not OOP.

5. An object is:

- (a) A blueprint for a class.
- (b) An instance of a class.
- (c) A function inside a class.
- (d) A data type in Python.

Answer: (b)

Explanation: Objects are instances of a class that store data and behavior.

Topic: Key Principles of OOP

6. What is encapsulation in OOP?

- (a) Hiding implementation details.
- (b) Using multiple inheritance.
- (c) Creating objects.
- (d) Sharing global variables.

Answer: (a)

Explanation: Encapsulation involves hiding the internal details of a class and exposing only the necessary parts.

7. How is encapsulation achieved in Python?

- (a) Using private and protected attributes.
- (b) Using loops.
- (c) Through functions.
- (d) Using global variables.

Answer: (a)

Explanation: Encapsulation is achieved using private (__) and protected (_) attributes in Python.

8. What does inheritance allow?

- (a) Creating classes that do not share functionality.
- (b) Reusing properties and methods of another class.

- (c) Overriding procedural programming.
- (d) Avoiding class creation.

Answer: (b)

Explanation: Inheritance enables one class (child) to inherit the properties and methods of another class (parent).

---

9. What is polymorphism?

- (a) Defining multiple classes.
- (b) Defining methods with the same name but different implementations.
- (c) Hiding data.
- (d) Using global variables.

Answer: (b)

Explanation: Polymorphism allows methods to have the same name but different behaviors, depending on the context.

---

10. Which OOP principle emphasizes hiding unnecessary details?

- (a) Abstraction.
- (b) Encapsulation.
- (c) Polymorphism.
- (d) Inheritance.

Answer: (a)

Explanation: Abstraction focuses on exposing only the necessary details and hiding the rest.

---

11. Which keyword is used to inherit a class in Python?

- (a) implement
- (b) extends
- (c) class
- (d) class Child(Parent)

Answer: (d)

Explanation: In Python, inheritance is achieved by passing the parent class name in parentheses after the child class name.

---

12. Which of the following is an example of polymorphism?

- (a) Class inheritance.

- (b) Method overriding.
- (c) Encapsulation.
- (d) Private methods.
  Answer: (b)
  Explanation: Method overriding allows derived classes to define a method with the same name as in the base class, demonstrating polymorphism.

13. What is method overloading?

- (a) Redefining a method in a derived class.
- (b) Using one method name to perform different tasks.
- (c) Defining multiple classes.
- (d) Using `super()` to access parent methods.
  Answer: (b)
  Explanation: Method overloading allows multiple methods with the same name but different arguments.

14. Which Python module helps implement abstraction?

- (a) abc
- (b) math
- (c) os
- (d) random
  Answer: (a)
  Explanation: The `abc` module in Python is used to create abstract base classes and methods.

15. Which OOP principle promotes reusability?

- (a) Polymorphism.
- (b) Inheritance.
- (c) Encapsulation.
- (d) Abstraction.
  Answer: (b)
  Explanation: Inheritance promotes reusability by allowing child classes to reuse the methods and properties of parent classes.

Additional Mixed Questions

16. What is the term for combining data and behavior in OOP?

- (a) Encapsulation.
- (b) Abstraction.
- (c) Polymorphism.
- (d) Inheritance.
  Answer: (a)

17. In OOP, a function defined inside a class is called:

- (a) A method.
- (b) An object.
- (c) A module.
- (d) An attribute.
  Answer: (a)

18. In Python, how is a private attribute defined?

- (a) By using an underscore before the variable name.
- (b) By using two underscores before the variable name.
- (c) By using the `private` keyword.
- (d) By using the `protected` keyword.
  Answer: (b)

19. What does the `super()` function do in Python?

- (a) Deletes the parent class.
- (b) Allows a child class to call methods of its parent class.
- (c) Stops inheritance.
- (d) Implements polymorphism.
  Answer: (b)

20. Which of the following is a valid class definition in Python?

- (a) `class MyClass:`
- (b) `def MyClass:`
- (c) `MyClass class:`
- (d) `Class MyClass:`
Answer: (a)

---

21. Which principle does the use of interfaces in Python promote?

- (a) Encapsulation.
- (b) Abstraction.
- (c) Polymorphism.
- (d) Inheritance.
Answer: (b)

---

22. What happens if a child class does not implement an abstract method?

- (a) It will throw an error.
- (b) It will use a default implementation.
- (c) The method will become private.
- (d) It will inherit a protected method.
Answer: (a)

---

23. Which keyword is used for method overriding in Python?

- (a) override
- (b) implement
- (c) No special keyword is needed.
- (d) extend
Answer: (c)

---

24. Which principle allows one interface to be used for multiple classes?

- (a) Abstraction.
- (b) Encapsulation.
- (c) Polymorphism.
- (d) Inheritance.
Answer: (c)

25. What is an attribute in Python OOP?

- (a) A function inside a class.
- (b) A variable that holds data specific to an object.
- (c) A keyword to define a class.
- (d) A decorator.
  Answer: (b)

CHAPTER 2: CLASSES AND OBJECTS

This chapter will explain the core concepts of classes and objects in Python. We will walk through defining and using classes, the importance of the __init__ method, understanding instance and class attributes, and provide practical examples of how these concepts come together.

1. Understanding Classes and Objects

Classes and **objects** are fundamental concepts in Object-Oriented Programming (OOP).

- **Class:** A class is a blueprint or template for creating objects. It defines the structure (attributes) and behavior (methods) that the objects created from it will have.

  Example:

  ```
  class Dog:
      def bark(self):
          print("Woof! Woof!")
  ```

  Here, `Dog` is a class that has a method `bark` that any instance (object) of the class `Dog` can use.

- **Object:** An object is an instance of a class. It is created from a class and can access the attributes and methods defined in that class.

  Example:

  ```
  my_dog = Dog()
  my_dog.bark()   # Output: Woof! Woof!
  ```

In this example, `my_dog` is an object of the class `Dog`.

2. Defining and Creating Classes

To define a class in Python, you use the `class` keyword, followed by the class name, which by convention is written in Pascal case (capitalized).

Syntax:

```
class ClassName:
    # class body
```

```
        pass
```

Example:

```
class Car:
    def drive(self):
        print("The car is moving.")
```

This `Car` class defines one method, `drive`, which prints a message when called.

Once a class is defined, you can create (instantiate) objects of that class.

---

3. Creating and Using Objects

To create an object from a class, you call the class like a function and pass the necessary arguments to the `__init__` method if required.

Syntax to create an object:

```
object_name = ClassName(arguments)
```

Example:

```
class Car:
    def __init__(self, brand, model):
        self.brand = brand
        self.model = model

    def display_info(self):
        print(f"Car: {self.brand} {self.model}")

# Creating an object of the Car class
my_car = Car("Toyota", "Corolla")
my_car.display_info()  # Output: Car: Toyota Corolla
```

Here:

- `my_car` is an object of the `Car` class.
- The `__init__` method initializes the `brand` and `model` attributes for the object.

You can create multiple objects from the same class, each with different data.

---

4. The `__init__` Method

The `__init__` method in Python is a special method used to initialize newly created objects of a class. It is commonly known as a **constructor**. This method is automatically invoked when an object is created from a class, and its primary role is to set up the initial state of the object by assigning values to its attributes.

Syntax of the `__init__` Method

The `__init__` method follows a standard syntax:

```
def __init__(self, parameter1, parameter2):
    self.attribute1 = parameter1
    self.attribute2 = parameter2
```

- `self`: Refers to the current instance of the class. It allows you to access instance variables and methods within the class.
- `parameter1`, `parameter2`: These are values passed during object creation to initialize the attributes of the class.
- `self.attribute1 = parameter1`: This line assigns the value of `parameter1` to the instance variable `attribute1`.

Example

Let's consider an example where we define a `Person` class that uses the `__init__` method:

```
class Person:
    def __init__(self, name, age):
        self.name = name   # Assigning the 'name' parameter to the
'name' attribute
        self.age = age     # Assigning the 'age' parameter to the 'age'
attribute

    def greet(self):
        print(f"Hello, my name is {self.name} and I am {self.age} years
old.")

# Creating an object of the 'Person' class
person1 = Person("Alice", 30)
person1.greet()   # Output: Hello, my name is Alice and I am 30 years
old.
```

Explanation of the Example:

1. **Class Definition**: The `Person` class has an `__init__` method that takes `name` and `age` as parameters and assigns them to the instance variables `self.name` and `self.age`.
2. **Object Creation**:

```
person1 = Person("Alice", 30)
```

- ○ When the object `person1` is created, Python automatically calls the `__init__` method.
- ○ The values "`Alice`" and 30 are passed to the `__init__` method.
- ○ These values are assigned to the `name` and `age` attributes of the `person1` object.

3. **Using the Object**:

```
person1.greet()   # Output: Hello, my name is Alice and I am 30
years old.
```

- ○ The `greet` method is called on the `person1` object, which accesses the `name` and `age` attributes and prints a greeting message.

Key Points About `__init__`:

- **Initialization**: The `__init__` method is responsible for initializing the object's state, i.e., assigning values to its attributes.
- **No Return Value**: The `__init__` method does not return any value (it implicitly returns `None`). Its only purpose is to set up the object's initial state.
- **Automatic Invocation**: When an object is created, Python automatically invokes the `__init__` method. You don't need to call it explicitly.

Why Use `__init__`?

The `__init__` method provides a clean and efficient way to initialize objects. It allows you to pass dynamic values when creating an object, ensuring that each object is initialized properly with the necessary data.

Example: Default Values in `__init__`

In some cases, you may want to set default values for certain attributes if they are not provided during object creation. This can be done using default arguments in the `__init__` method.

```
class Person:
    def __init__(self, name="Unknown", age=0):
        self.name = name
        self.age = age

    def greet(self):
        print(f"Hello, my name is {self.name} and I am {self.age} years
old.")

# Creating an object with specified values
```

```
person1 = Person("Alice", 30)
person1.greet()   # Output: Hello, my name is Alice and I am 30 years
old.

# Creating an object with default values
person2 = Person()
person2.greet()   # Output: Hello, my name is Unknown and I am 0 years
old.
```

In this example, the `name` and `age` parameters in the `__init__` method have default values (`"Unknown"` and `0`), so if no values are passed during object creation, these defaults will be used.

5. Class vs. Instance Attributes

In Python, class attributes and instance attributes are used to store data. Understanding the difference between them is crucial in object-oriented programming (OOP) as they behave differently in terms of storage and usage. Let's break down the differences and see examples for better clarity.

1. Instance Attributes

- **Definition**: Instance attributes are specific to an object (instance) of a class. They are defined inside the `__init__` method using the `self` keyword, making them unique to each instance.
- **Characteristics**:
  - Each object (instance) can have its own value for an instance attribute.
  - Instance attributes are created and initialized when an object is instantiated.
  - They are accessed using `self.attribute_name` within methods.

Example of Instance Attributes

```
class Student:
    def __init__(self, name, grade):
        self.name = name  # instance attribute
        self.grade = grade  # instance attribute

# Creating instances (objects) of Student class
student1 = Student("John", "A")
student2 = Student("Jane", "B")

# Accessing instance attributes
print(student1.name)   # Output: John
print(student1.grade)   # Output: A

print(student2.name)    # Output: Jane
```

```
print(student2.grade)   # Output: B
```

Explanation:

- In this example, `name` and `grade` are instance attributes.
- `student1` and `student2` have their own `name` and `grade` values, making them unique to each instance.
- `student1.name` is "John", and `student2.name` is "Jane". Similarly, their grades are also unique.

---

2. Class Attributes

- **Definition**: Class attributes are shared by all instances (objects) of a class. They are defined inside the class, but outside of any methods, and they belong to the class rather than to any particular instance.
- **Characteristics**:
  - All instances of the class share the same value for a class attribute.
  - They are defined directly in the class body.
  - Class attributes are typically used for properties or data that are common across all instances of the class.

Example of Class Attributes

```
class Student:
    school_name = "ABC High School"  # class attribute

    def __init__(self, name, grade):
        self.name = name  # instance attribute
        self.grade = grade  # instance attribute

# Creating instances (objects) of Student class
student1 = Student("John", "A")
student2 = Student("Jane", "B")

# Accessing class attribute
print(student1.school_name)   # Output: ABC High School
print(student2.school_name)   # Output: ABC High School
```

Explanation:

- `school_name` is a **class attribute**. It's shared across all instances of the `Student` class.
- Even though `student1` and `student2` have different `name` and `grade` values (instance attributes), they both refer to the same `school_name` class attribute, which is "ABC High School".

- Both `student1.school_name` and `student2.school_name` return the same value, `"ABC High School"`, because class attributes are shared.

Key Differences Between Class and Instance Attributes

Aspect	Instance Attributes	Class Attributes
Defined	Inside the `__init__` method, using `self`	Directly inside the class body
Scope	Specific to an instance of the class	Shared across all instances of the class
Access	Accessed using `self.attribute_name`	Accessed using `ClassName.attribute_name` or `self.attribute_name`
Initialization	Initialized for each object when created	Initialized once for the class, not per object
Modification	Can be modified individually for each object	Modifying a class attribute affects all instances, unless overridden in the instance

Practical Example: Modifying Class vs. Instance Attributes

```python
class Car:
    # Class attribute
    manufacturer = "Toyota"

    def __init__(self, model, year):
        # Instance attributes
        self.model = model
        self.year = year

# Creating instances (objects) of Car class
car1 = Car("Corolla", 2020)
car2 = Car("Camry", 2021)

# Accessing class attribute
print(car1.manufacturer)   # Output: Toyota
print(car2.manufacturer)   # Output: Toyota

# Modifying instance attributes
car1.year = 2022
print(car1.year)   # Output: 2022
print(car2.year)   # Output: 2021

# Modifying class attribute
```

```
Car.manufacturer = "Honda"
print(car1.manufacturer)  # Output: Honda
print(car2.manufacturer)  # Output: Honda
```

Explanation:

- Initially, both `car1` and `car2` share the same `manufacturer` class attribute, which is `"Toyota"`.
- After modifying the `manufacturer` class attribute (i.e., `Car.manufacturer = "Honda"`), it affects both `car1` and `car2`, since class attributes are shared by all instances of the class.
- However, when we modify the `year` instance attribute for `car1`, it does not affect `car2`, since instance attributes are unique to each object.

6. Practical Examples

Example 1: Simple Class with Methods

Let's create a simple `Person` class that uses instance and class attributes.

```
class Person:
    species = "Homo sapiens"  # class attribute

    def __init__(self, name, age):
        self.name = name  # instance attribute
        self.age = age  # instance attribute

    def greet(self):
        print(f"Hello, my name is {self.name} and I am {self.age} years
old.")

# Creating objects
person1 = Person("Alice", 30)
person2 = Person("Bob", 25)

person1.greet()  # Output: Hello, my name is Alice and I am 30 years
old.
person2.greet()  # Output: Hello, my name is Bob and I am 25 years old.

print(person1.species)  # Output: Homo sapiens
print(person2.species)  # Output: Homo sapiens
```

In this example:

- `species` is a class attribute, shared among all `Person` objects.
- `name` and `age` are instance attributes, unique to each object.
- The method `greet` uses both instance attributes (`name`, `age`) to output a personalized greeting.

Example 2: Using Class and Instance Attributes for Banking

Let's create a `BankAccount` class to show how both class and instance attributes are used in a real-world scenario.

```
class BankAccount:
    bank_name = "XYZ Bank"  # class attribute

    def __init__(self, account_holder, balance):
        self.account_holder = account_holder  # instance attribute
        self.balance = balance  # instance attribute

    def deposit(self, amount):
        self.balance += amount
        print(f"Deposited {amount}. New balance: {self.balance}")

    def withdraw(self, amount):
        if self.balance >= amount:
            self.balance -= amount
            print(f"Withdrew {amount}. New balance: {self.balance}")
        else:
            print("Insufficient balance.")

# Creating objects
account1 = BankAccount("Alice", 1000)
account2 = BankAccount("Bob", 500)

account1.deposit(200)   # Deposited 200. New balance: 1200
account1.withdraw(100)  # Withdrew 100. New balance: 1100
account2.withdraw(600)  # Insufficient balance.

print(account1.bank_name)   # Output: XYZ Bank
print(account2.bank_name)   # Output: XYZ Bank
```

Here:

- `bank_name` is a class attribute (same for all accounts).
- `account_holder` and `balance` are instance attributes, specific to each bank account.
- Methods like `deposit` and `withdraw` modify the instance attributes (`balance`), demonstrating the interaction of object behavior with attributes.

Example 3: Employee Class with Department Information

This example demonstrates using instance attributes for personal details and class attributes for department-wide information.

```
class Employee:
    company_name = "TechCorp"  # class attribute

    def __init__(self, name, position):
        self.name = name  # instance attribute
        self.position = position  # instance attribute
```

```python
    def display_info(self):
        print(f"{self.name} works as a {self.position} at
{Employee.company_name}.")

# Creating objects
employee1 = Employee("Alice", "Software Engineer")
employee2 = Employee("Bob", "Project Manager")

employee1.display_info()   # Output: Alice works as a Software Engineer
at TechCorp.
employee2.display_info()   # Output: Bob works as a Project Manager at
TechCorp.

print(employee1.company_name)   # Output: TechCorp
print(employee2.company_name)   # Output: TechCorp
```

Explanation:

- `company_name` is a class attribute, shared by all employees.
- `name` and `position` are instance attributes, unique to each employee.

Example 4: Car Class with Static and Instance Attributes

Here we demonstrate how to use class attributes for common car data (like the manufacturer) and instance attributes for unique data (like the model and year).

```python
class Car:
    manufacturer = "Toyota"   # class attribute

    def __init__(self, model, year):
        self.model = model   # instance attribute
        self.year = year   # instance attribute

    def car_info(self):
        print(f"{self.year} {self.manufacturer} {self.model}")

# Creating objects
car1 = Car("Corolla", 2020)
car2 = Car("Camry", 2021)

car1.car_info()   # Output: 2020 Toyota Corolla
car2.car_info()   # Output: 2021 Toyota Camry

print(car1.manufacturer)   # Output: Toyota
print(car2.manufacturer)   # Output: Toyota
```

Explanation:

- `manufacturer` is a class attribute, common across all cars.
- `model` and `year` are instance attributes, specific to each car.

Example 5: Library Class with Book Count and Title Information

This example uses class attributes for library-wide data and instance attributes for individual book data.

```
class Library:
    total_books = 0  # class attribute

    def __init__(self, title, author):
        self.title = title  # instance attribute
        self.author = author  # instance attribute
        Library.total_books += 1

    def book_info(self):
        print(f"Book: {self.title}, Author: {self.author}")

# Creating objects
book1 = Library("Python Programming", "John Doe")
book2 = Library("Data Science Essentials", "Jane Smith")

book1.book_info()  # Output: Book: Python Programming, Author: John Doe
book2.book_info()  # Output: Book: Data Science Essentials, Author:
Jane Smith

print(Library.total_books)  # Output: 2
```

Explanation:

- `total_books` is a class attribute, tracking the total number of books across the library.
- `title` and `author` are instance attributes, specific to each book.

Example 6: Animal Class with Species and Name Information

This example demonstrates using class attributes for species-wide data and instance attributes for individual animal names.

```
class Animal:
    species = "Unknown"  # class attribute

    def __init__(self, name):
        self.name = name  # instance attribute

    def display_info(self):
        print(f"{self.name} is a {self.species}.")

# Creating objects
animal1 = Animal("Lion")
animal2 = Animal("Elephant")

animal1.display_info()  # Output: Lion is a Unknown.
```

```
animal2.display_info()  # Output: Elephant is a Unknown.

# Changing the class attribute
Animal.species = "Mammal"

animal1.display_info()  # Output: Lion is a Mammal.
animal2.display_info()  # Output: Elephant is a Mammal.
```

Explanation:

- `species` is a class attribute, which can be shared across instances.
- `name` is an instance attribute, unique for each animal.

Example 7: Student Class with Class and Instance Attributes

This example shows how both class and instance attributes are used in a student record system.

```
class Student:
    school_name = "Sunrise High"  # class attribute

    def __init__(self, name, grade):
        self.name = name  # instance attribute
        self.grade = grade  # instance attribute

    def display_info(self):
        print(f"{self.name} is in grade {self.grade} at
{Student.school_name}.")

# Creating objects
student1 = Student("Alice", "A")
student2 = Student("Bob", "B")

student1.display_info()  # Output: Alice is in grade A at Sunrise High.
student2.display_info()  # Output: Bob is in grade B at Sunrise High.

print(student1.school_name)  # Output: Sunrise High
print(student2.school_name)  # Output: Sunrise High
```

Explanation:

- `school_name` is a class attribute shared across all students.
- `name` and `grade` are instance attributes, specific to each student.

Example 8: Shape Class with Area Calculation

This example demonstrates a `Shape` class where area calculations are dependent on specific object types.

```
class Shape:
    def __init__(self, name):
        self.name = name  # instance attribute

    def area(self):
        return 0  # Default area for general shapes

class Circle(Shape):
    def __init__(self, name, radius):
        super().__init__(name)  # Calling the parent class __init__
        self.radius = radius  # instance attribute

    def area(self):
        return 3.14 * (self.radius ** 2)

class Rectangle(Shape):
    def __init__(self, name, length, width):
        super().__init__(name)  # Calling the parent class __init__
        self.length = length  # instance attribute
        self.width = width  # instance attribute

    def area(self):
        return self.length * self.width

# Creating objects
circle = Circle("Circle", 5)
rectangle = Rectangle("Rectangle", 4, 6)

print(f"Area of {circle.name}: {circle.area()}")  # Output: Area of
Circle: 78.5
print(f"Area of {rectangle.name}: {rectangle.area()}")  # Output: Area
of Rectangle: 24
```

Explanation:

- `name` is an instance attribute for all shapes, inherited from the `Shape` class.
- `radius`, `length`, and `width` are instance attributes specific to their respective subclasses (`Circle` and `Rectangle`).
- The `area()` method is overridden in the subclasses to calculate the specific area based on instance attributes.

Example 9: Library System with Class and Instance Attributes

This example demonstrates a library system using both class and instance attributes.

```
class Library:
    library_name = "City Library"  # class attribute

    def __init__(self, book_title, author):
        self.book_title = book_title  # instance attribute
        self.author = author  # instance attribute
```

```
    def book_info(self):
        print(f"'{self.book_title}' by {self.author} is available at
{Library.library_name}.")

# Creating objects
book1 = Library("1984", "George Orwell")
book2 = Library("To Kill a Mockingbird", "Harper Lee")

book1.book_info()  # Output: '1984' by George Orwell is available at
City Library.
book2.book_info()  # Output: 'To Kill a Mockingbird' by Harper Lee is
available at City Library.

print(Library.library_name)  # Output: City Library
```

Explanation:

- `library_name` is a class attribute shared across all books.
- `book_title` and `author` are instance attributes, unique to each book.

Example 10: Product Class with Stock Management

This example demonstrates how both class and instance attributes are used in a product inventory management system.

```
class Product:
    store_name = "TechStore"  # class attribute

    def __init__(self, product_name, price, stock_quantity):
        self.product_name = product_name  # instance attribute
        self.price = price  # instance attribute
        self.stock_quantity = stock_quantity  # instance attribute

    def display_info(self):
        print(f"Product: {self.product_name}, Price: ${self.price},
Stock Quantity: {self.stock_quantity}")

    def update_stock(self, quantity_sold):
        if quantity_sold <= self.stock_quantity:
            self.stock_quantity -= quantity_sold
            print(f"Sold {quantity_sold} {self.product_name}(s).
Remaining stock: {self.stock_quantity}")
        else:
            print(f"Not enough stock for {self.product_name}. Only
{self.stock_quantity} left.")

# Creating objects
product1 = Product("Laptop", 999.99, 50)
product2 = Product("Smartphone", 599.99, 100)

product1.display_info()  # Output: Product: Laptop, Price: $999.99,
Stock Quantity: 50
```

```
product2.display_info()   # Output: Product: Smartphone, Price: $599.99,
Stock Quantity: 100

product1.update_stock(10)   # Output: Sold 10 Laptop(s). Remaining
stock: 40
product2.update_stock(150)   # Output: Not enough stock for Smartphone.
Only 100 left.

print(product1.store_name)   # Output: TechStore
print(product2.store_name)   # Output: TechStore
```

Explanation:

- `store_name` is a class attribute, shared across all products.
- `product_name`, `price`, and `stock_quantity` are instance attributes, specific to each product.
- The `update_stock` method modifies the `stock_quantity` for each instance, demonstrating how instance attributes can be updated.

MCQ

1. Understanding Classes and Objects

1. **What is a class in Python?**
   - o a) A blueprint for creating objects
   - o b) A collection of functions
   - o c) A data structure for storing values
   - o d) A method to execute code
   - o **Answer:** a) A blueprint for creating objects
2. **What is an object in Python?**
   - o a) A function within a class
   - o b) An instance of a class
   - o c) A method in a class
   - o d) A class variable
   - o **Answer:** b) An instance of a class
3. **Which of the following is true about an object?**
   - o a) An object is a class
   - o b) An object is an instance of a class
   - o c) An object cannot have attributes
   - o d) An object can only have one method
   - o **Answer:** b) An object is an instance of a class
4. **What does the self parameter refer to in a class method?**
   - o a) The class itself
   - o b) The calling object instance
   - o c) The constructor of the class
   - o d) The method being defined
   - o **Answer:** b) The calling object instance

5. **Which of the following is not an advantage of OOP?**
   - a) Code reusability
   - b) Encapsulation
   - c) Inheritance
   - d) Slow performance
   - **Answer:** d) Slow performance

---

2. Defining and Creating Classes

6. **How do you define a class in Python?**
   - a) `class ClassName {}`
   - b) `def ClassName():`
   - c) `class ClassName:`
   - d) `class ClassName[]:`
   - **Answer:** c) `class ClassName:`

7. **Which of the following is a valid class definition in Python?**
   - a) `class Dog() { }`
   - b) `class Dog:`
   - c) `def class Dog:`
   - d) `function class Dog():`
   - **Answer:** b) `class Dog:`

8. **In Python, what is the default name for the first method in a class?**
   - a) `start()`
   - b) `__init__()`
   - c) `__main__()`
   - d) `__new__()`
   - **Answer:** b) `__init__()`

9. **Which of the following is used to initialize the attributes of a class?**
   - a) `__new__()`
   - b) `__call__()`
   - c) `__init__()`
   - d) `__start__()`
   - **Answer:** c) `__init__()`

10. **Which of the following code will create an instance of a class named `Car`?**
    - a) `car1 = Car()`
    - b) `Car() = car1`
    - c) `Car = car1()`
    - d) `car1 = new Car()`
    - **Answer:** a) `car1 = Car()`

3. Creating and Using Objects

11. **What is required to create an object of a class in Python?**
    - o a) The class must have a constructor method
    - o b) The class must have at least one method
    - o c) The class must be instantiated by calling it as a function
    - o d) The class must inherit from another class
    - o **Answer:** a) The class must have a constructor method

12. **How do you call a method** `greet()` **from an object** `person1`**?**
    - o a) `person1.greet()`
    - o b) `greet(person1)`
    - o c) `greet.person1()`
    - o d) `person1->greet()`
    - o **Answer:** a) `person1.greet()`

13. **What will be the output of the following code?**

```
class Student:
    def __init__(self, name):
        self.name = name
    def greet(self):
        print(f"Hello, {self.name}")

student1 = Student("Alice")
student1.greet()
```

    - o a) `Hello, None`
    - o b) `Hello, Alice`
    - o c) `Hello, student1`
    - o d) Error
    - o **Answer:** b) `Hello, Alice`

14. **Which of the following statements creates a new object from the class** `Car`**?**
    - o a) `Car = Car()`
    - o b) `my_car = Car()`
    - o c) `Car()`
    - o d) `new Car = Car()`
    - o **Answer:** b) `my_car = Car()`

15. **What will happen if you attempt to access an attribute of an object that doesn't exist?**
    - o a) The program will stop
    - o b) A new attribute will be created
    - o c) It will raise an AttributeError
    - o d) It will return `None`
    - o **Answer:** c) It will raise an AttributeError

4. The __init__ Method

16. **What is the purpose of the __init__() method in a class?**
    - o a) It initializes the object's attributes
    - o b) It runs every time an object is used
    - o c) It is the method used to destroy an object
    - o d) It defines the class behavior
    - o **Answer:** a) It initializes the object's attributes

17. **What does `self` represent in the __init__() method?**
    - o a) It refers to the class
    - o b) It refers to the instance of the object
    - o c) It refers to a static variable
    - o d) It refers to a method
    - o **Answer:** b) It refers to the instance of the object

18. **What will the following code output?**

```
class Animal:
    def __init__(self, name):
        self.name = name

    def speak(self):
        print(f"{self.name} says Hello!")

dog = Animal("Dog")
dog.speak()
```

    - o a) `Dog says Hello!`
    - o b) `None says Hello!`
    - o c) `Dog Hello!`
    - o d) Error
    - o **Answer:** a) `Dog says Hello!`

19. **Which of the following is correct for using the __init__() method in a class?**
    - o a) It does not take parameters
    - o b) It must take only one parameter `self`
    - o c) It must be called explicitly to initialize attributes
    - o d) It is automatically called when an object is created
    - o **Answer:** d) It is automatically called when an object is created

20. **What will happen if __init__() is not defined in a class?**
    - o a) The class cannot be used
    - o b) Python will automatically define the __init__() method
    - o c) The object will not be created
    - o d) An error will occur
    - o **Answer:** b) Python will automatically define the __init__() method

5. Class vs. Instance Attributes

21. **What is an instance attribute in Python?**
    - o   a) A variable that is shared by all instances of the class
    - o   b) A variable that is specific to an instance of the class
    - o   c) A method of the class
    - o   d) A special attribute that cannot be modified
    - o   **Answer:** b) A variable that is specific to an instance of the class

22. **Which of the following is a class attribute in Python?**
    - o   a) `self.name`
    - o   b) `name = "John"`
    - o   c) `def __init__(self):`
    - o   d) `self.__name`
    - o   **Answer:** b) `name = "John"`

23. **Which of the following is true about class attributes?**
    - o   a) They are unique to each object
    - o   b) They are shared among all instances of the class
    - o   c) They are created in the `__init__()` method
    - o   d) They cannot be accessed directly
    - o   **Answer:** b) They are shared among all instances of the class

24. **If a class has an attribute `color = "blue"`, how can we change the color for a specific object?**
    - o   a) `object.color = "red"`
    - o   b) `object.color = blue`
    - o   c) `object.set_color("red")`
    - o   d) `object.change_color("red")`
    - o   **Answer:** a) `object.color = "red"`

25. **What will be the output of the following code?**

```
class Car:
    brand = "Toyota"  # class attribute

    def __init__(self, model):
        self.model = model  # instance attribute

car1 = Car("Corolla")
car2 = Car("Camry")

print(car1.brand)
print(car2.model)
```

    - o   a) `Toyota Camry`
    - o   b) `Toyota Corolla`
    - o   c) `Toyota Camry`
    - o   d) `None Camry`
    - o   **Answer:** c) `Toyota Camry`

Conclusion

Understanding classes and objects is the cornerstone of mastering Object-Oriented Programming in Python. By defining classes and creating objects, you can organize and structure your code more effectively. The __init__ method is key for initializing objects, while instance and class attributes help in managing data that belongs either to individual objects or the class as a whole. These concepts form the foundation of many real-world Python applications.

CHAPTER 3: ENCAPSULATION

Encapsulation is one of the fundamental concepts in Object-Oriented Programming (OOP) and refers to the bundling of data (attributes) and methods (functions) that operate on the data within a single unit or class. Encapsulation helps protect the integrity of an object by restricting access to some of its components, which can prevent unintended interference and misuse of its attributes.

1. Understanding Encapsulation

Encapsulation is one of the four fundamental principles of Object-Oriented Programming (OOP), alongside inheritance, polymorphism, and abstraction. It refers to the technique of bundling the data (attributes) and methods (functions) that operate on the data into a single unit or class. The main purpose of encapsulation is to control access to the internal state of an object and restrict access to the implementation details.

By encapsulating the data and methods within a class, we can prevent direct access to the data and ensure that it is modified or accessed only in controlled ways through specific methods. This results in more secure, modular, and maintainable code.

Key Concepts in Encapsulation

1. **Private Attributes**
   Private attributes are those variables within a class that are intended to be used internally by the class only and should not be accessed or modified directly from outside the class. In Python, private attributes are conventionally denoted by a double underscore (__) before the attribute name, signaling that these are intended to be private.

   For example:

   ```
   class Person:
       def __init__(self, name, age):
           self.__name = name  # Private attribute
           self.__age = age  # Private attribute
   ```

   In the example above, __name and __age are private attributes. They are only meant to be accessed or modified inside the class and cannot be accessed directly from outside.

2. **Public Attributes**
   Public attributes are those that can be accessed directly from outside the class.

These are not hidden and can be modified freely, unlike private attributes. Public attributes are defined without the double underscore (__) prefix.

For example:

```
class Person:
    def __init__(self, name, age):
        self.name = name  # Public attribute
        self.age = age  # Public attribute
```

Here, `name` and `age` are public attributes, which can be accessed or modified directly from outside the class.

How Encapsulation Works in Python

In Python, encapsulation is not enforced strictly by the language itself, as Python relies on a principle called *"we are all consenting adults"*. This means that Python uses naming conventions to indicate the intended visibility of an attribute or method, rather than enforcing access restrictions. Despite this, encapsulation can still be achieved using naming conventions and tools like getter and setter methods, or the `@property` decorator.

Private Attributes and Methods

In Python, a double underscore prefix (__) makes an attribute or method private. This doesn't make it truly inaccessible, but it prevents accidental access by altering its name internally (name mangling). For instance, the private attribute __name can still be accessed from outside using the following syntax:

```
person = Person("Alice", 30)
print(person._Person__name)  # Accessing private attribute from outside
```

Although this is possible, it is discouraged to use private attributes in this way, as it breaks the encapsulation.

Benefits of Encapsulation

1. **Data Protection**

   Encapsulation provides a mechanism for data protection by ensuring that an object's internal state is not modified inappropriately. By using private attributes and providing controlled access to them via getter and setter methods, you can prevent accidental changes to the state of the object.

For example, in a BankAccount class, we might want to ensure that a bank account balance cannot be directly set to a negative value:

```
class BankAccount:
    def __init__(self, balance):
        self.__balance = balance  # Private attribute

    @property
    def balance(self):
        return self.__balance

    @balance.setter
    def balance(self, value):
        if value >= 0:
            self.__balance = value
        else:
            print("Balance cannot be negative!")
```

By using the setter method, we can ensure that the balance cannot be set to a negative value, thus protecting the internal state.

2. **Abstraction**

Encapsulation also contributes to **abstraction**. Abstraction is the concept of hiding complex implementation details and exposing only the necessary features. Through encapsulation, the user interacts with an object via a simplified interface, without needing to understand the internal workings of the class.

For example, a car's engine can be encapsulated within the Car class. The driver doesn't need to know how the engine works internally, but can still drive the car by interacting with the public methods such as start_engine(), accelerate(), and brake().

```
class Car:
    def __init__(self):
        self.__engine_status = "off"

    def start_engine(self):
        self.__engine_status = "on"
        print("Engine started.")

    def stop_engine(self):
        self.__engine_status = "off"
        print("Engine stopped.")
```

The driver doesn't need to know the intricate details of how the engine works; they simply interact with the start_engine or stop_engine methods.

3. **Code Organization**

Encapsulation promotes better **code organization** by grouping related data and methods together within a class. This makes the code more modular and easier to maintain. When the data and functions that operate on the data are kept together, it leads to more logical and intuitive design.

For instance, in a Student class, the student's name, ID, and grades can be bundled together with the methods that operate on them, making it easy to manage and maintain the student's information.

```
class Student:
    def __init__(self, name, student_id, grades):
        self.__name = name
        self.__student_id = student_id
        self.__grades = grades

    def get_grades(self):
        return self.__grades

    def update_grades(self, new_grades):
        self.__grades = new_grades
```

The `Student` class encapsulates all attributes related to a student, and methods like `get_grades` and `update_grades` operate on these attributes. This structure ensures that all student data is accessed in an organized manner.

Real-World Example of Encapsulation

Consider a **Social Media Application** where a user's personal information needs to be kept private and secure. Using encapsulation, you can protect sensitive data such as passwords and email addresses by making them private, while allowing controlled access to them through getter and setter methods.

```
class UserProfile:
    def __init__(self, username, email, password):
        self.__username = username
        self.__email = email
        self.__password = password

    # Getter method for email
    @property
    def email(self):
        return self.__email

    # Setter method for email
    @email.setter
    def email(self, new_email):
        self.__email = new_email
```

```
# Getter method for password
@property
def password(self):
    return self.__password

# Setter method for password (with validation)
@password.setter
def password(self, new_password):
    if len(new_password) >= 8:
        self.__password = new_password
    else:
        print("Password must be at least 8 characters long.")

# Example usage
user = UserProfile("john_doe", "john@example.com", "securepass")
print(user.email)   # Output: john@example.com
user.password = "newpass"   # Valid password change
print(user.password)   # Output: newpass
```

In the above example, the email and password are protected using encapsulation. Direct access to these attributes is not allowed; instead, they can only be accessed or modified through getter and setter methods, ensuring that passwords follow certain rules (e.g., minimum length).

2. Private and Public Attributes

In Python, you can define attributes (variables) inside a class as either **public** or **private**.

- **Public Attributes:** These are the attributes that are accessible from anywhere, both inside and outside the class.

  Example of public attribute:

```
class Person:
    def __init__(self, name, age):
        self.name = name   # Public attribute
        self.age = age   # Public attribute
```

- **Private Attributes:** These attributes are intended to be accessed only within the class. In Python, private attributes are indicated by a double underscore (__) before the attribute name.

  Example of private attribute:

```
class Person:
    def __init__(self, name, age):
        self.__name = name   # Private attribute
        self.__age = age   # Private attribute
```

Why use private attributes?

- Prevent direct modification of attributes from outside the class.
- Encapsulate sensitive data and control access to it through getter and setter methods.

---

3. Getter and Setter Methods

Getter and setter methods are essential tools in object-oriented programming, specifically in the context of **encapsulation**. These methods provide controlled access to private attributes of a class, allowing us to retrieve (get) or modify (set) the value of an attribute, while maintaining the integrity and security of the object's state.

In Python, although direct access to an attribute is possible, it is recommended to use getter and setter methods when dealing with private or protected data. This provides a layer of control and validation, making the code more secure, reliable, and easier to maintain.

What are Getter and Setter Methods?

1. **Getter Method**

   A **getter** method is a function that retrieves the value of a private attribute. It provides a controlled way to access the value of a private attribute, which would otherwise be hidden from the outside world due to encapsulation.

   In Python, the getter method typically follows a pattern like `get_<attribute_name>`, where `<attribute_name>` corresponds to the private attribute name, without the leading double underscore (__).

   Example:

   ```python
   def get_name(self):
       return self.__name
   ```

   In this example, `get_name` is the getter method for the private attribute `__name`.

2. **Setter Method**

   A **setter** method is a function that sets or modifies the value of a private attribute. It allows controlled modification, and often includes validation logic to ensure that only valid data is assigned to the attribute.

A setter typically follows a pattern like `set_<attribute_name>`, and it allows you to set the value of a private attribute while ensuring that any rules or constraints are followed.

Example:

```
def set_name(self, name):
    self.__name = name
```

In this example, `set_name` is the setter method that modifies the private attribute `__name`.

Example of Getter and Setter Methods

Here's a simple class example using getter and setter methods to access and modify private attributes:

```
class Person:
    def __init__(self, name, age):
        self.__name = name   # Private attribute
        self.__age = age   # Private attribute

    # Getter method for name
    def get_name(self):
        return self.__name

    # Setter method for name
    def set_name(self, name):
        self.__name = name

    # Getter method for age
    def get_age(self):
        return self.__age

    # Setter method for age with validation
    def set_age(self, age):
        if age > 0:
            self.__age = age
        else:
            print("Age must be positive.")
```

In the above class:

- The __name and __age attributes are private, and cannot be accessed directly from outside the class.
- We use **getter** methods like `get_name()` and `get_age()` to retrieve the values of these attributes.
- We use **setter** methods like `set_name()` and `set_age()` to modify the values of these attributes.

Usage of Getter and Setter Methods

Let's demonstrate how we can use the getter and setter methods with an example:

```
person = Person("Alice", 25)

# Accessing the name using the getter method
print(person.get_name())   # Output: Alice

# Changing the name using the setter method
person.set_name("Bob")
print(person.get_name())   # Output: Bob

# Modifying the age using the setter method
person.set_age(30)
print(person.get_age())   # Output: 30

# Trying to set an invalid age (negative value)
person.set_age(-5)   # Output: Age must be positive.
```

In this example:

- We first create a `Person` object `person` with name "Alice" and age 25.
- We then use the getter method `get_name()` to retrieve the name, which outputs "Alice".
- We use the setter method `set_name("Bob")` to change the name to "Bob", and `get_name()` retrieves the updated value.
- We use the setter method `set_age(30)` to modify the age, and `get_age()` confirms the change.
- Finally, we try to set an invalid age of -5 using `set_age(-5)`, but the setter method includes validation that prevents this, outputting "Age must be positive."

Benefits of Using Getter and Setter Methods

1. **Data Validation**

   One of the primary advantages of using getter and setter methods is **data validation**. You can ensure that any value being assigned to an attribute meets certain criteria or constraints before allowing it to be modified. For example, in the `set_age()` method above, we validated that age cannot be negative, which helps maintain the integrity of the object's state.

   Benefits of validation include:

   - Preventing invalid or inconsistent data.

- o Enforcing business rules (e.g., non-negative age).
- o Enhancing data integrity and security.

2. Encapsulation

By using getter and setter methods, you hide the internal workings of the class from external code. This means you can change the implementation of how an attribute is stored or calculated without affecting the external interface of the class. This is a key advantage of **encapsulation**, as it helps in abstracting away complexity and protecting the internal state.

For example, if the `age` attribute was initially stored as a simple integer, but later you decided to store it as a more complex object (like `DateOfBirth`), the outside code using `get_age()` and `set_age()` wouldn't need to be modified.

3. Control Over Attribute Access

Getter and setter methods give you full control over how attributes are accessed and modified. You can:

- o Add logic to modify the data before returning or setting it.
- o Ensure attributes are accessed or modified only in specific ways, preventing undesirable behavior or bugs.
- o Implement side effects, such as logging or triggering other actions when an attribute is modified.

For example, you could modify the setter for `name` to ensure it always capitalizes the first letter:

```
def set_name(self, name):
    self.__name = name.capitalize()
```

4. Read-Only and Write-Only Attributes

By using getter and setter methods, you can easily create **read-only** or **write-only** attributes. For instance, if you only want an attribute to be accessed but not modified, you can create a getter method without a corresponding setter:

```
def get_name(self):
    return self.__name
```

Conversely, if you only want to allow writing an attribute (but not reading), you can provide a setter without a getter.

5. Future Flexibility

Getter and setter methods provide flexibility in how the data is accessed and modified in the future. If you need to change the way data is stored or perform additional checks when modifying an attribute, you can modify the setter or getter without affecting external code that relies on them.

4. Using @property Decorator

In Python, the `@property` decorator is a powerful feature that allows you to create properties, providing an elegant and Pythonic way to define getter and setter methods. The `@property` decorator turns a method into an attribute-like access mechanism, so you can access the value as if it were a normal attribute rather than a method. This makes the code more readable and intuitive.

The `@property` decorator simplifies the process of using getter and setter methods while keeping the flexibility of encapsulation and validation.

What is a Property in Python?

A **property** in Python is a special type of attribute that is managed by getter, setter, and deleter methods. Using the `@property` decorator, we can define methods that act like attributes, enabling access to an attribute via a method call, but without needing to explicitly call it like a method. This allows you to still control how the attribute is accessed or modified, but in a clean and intuitive way.

How Does @property Work?

1. **Getter Method with @property**
   The `@property` decorator turns a method into a "getter" for a property. This method can be accessed as an attribute, without explicitly calling it like a function.
2. **Setter Method with @property_name.setter**
   The setter method is used to modify the value of the attribute. To define a setter, you use the same name as the property method and decorate it with `@property_name.setter`.
3. **Using @property for Read/Write Access**
   The `@property` decorator allows you to easily access and modify attributes as if they were public attributes, while still keeping control over how data is handled internally.

Example Using the @property Decorator

Here is an example that demonstrates the use of `@property` and `@property_name.setter` in Python:

```python
class Person:
    def __init__(self, name, age):
        self.__name = name
        self.__age = age

    # Getter method using @property
    @property
    def name(self):
        return self.__name

    # Setter method using @name.setter
    @name.setter
    def name(self, name):
        self.__name = name

    # Getter method using @property for age
    @property
    def age(self):
        return self.__age

    # Setter method for age with validation
    @age.setter
    def age(self, age):
        if age > 0:
            self.__age = age
        else:
            print("Age must be positive.")
```

Explanation of the Example

1. **The `__init__` Method:**
   The constructor method initializes the __name and __age private attributes when a `Person` object is created.
2. **The `name` Property:**
   - The method `name` is decorated with `@property`, which makes it accessible like an attribute, allowing us to use `person.name` to retrieve the value of __name.
   - The `name` setter (`@name.setter`) allows us to modify the value of __name using `person.name = new_value`.
3. **The `age` Property:**
   - The method `age` is also decorated with `@property`, allowing access to __age using `person.age`.
   - The `age` setter includes a validation check to ensure the age is positive before updating the value of __age.

Usage of the @property Decorator

```
person = Person("Alice", 25)

# Accessing the name via getter
print(person.name)   # Output: Alice

# Setting the name via setter
person.name = "Bob"
print(person.name)   # Output: Bob

# Setting the age via setter
person.age = 30
print(person.age)   # Output: 30

# Trying to set an invalid age (negative value)
person.age = -5   # Output: Age must be positive.
```

In this usage example:

- We access the `name` and `age` as if they were regular attributes, even though they are actually handled by getter and setter methods.
- The `name` and `age` properties can be modified and accessed directly using the syntax `person.name` and `person.age`, which is more intuitive and cleaner than calling getter and setter methods explicitly.

Advantages of @property

1. **Simplifies Code:**
   - The `@property` decorator provides an easy way to define getter and setter methods while maintaining the simplicity of attribute-like access. You don't have to explicitly call methods, which makes the code easier to read and use.
2. **Cleaner and More Intuitive Code:**
   - Using `@property`, the code looks cleaner because you don't have to call getter and setter methods explicitly. It feels like you're working with regular attributes rather than methods, which improves code readability and intuitiveness.
3. **Encapsulation with Controlled Access:**
   - Despite the property appearing like an attribute, it is still controlled by getter and setter methods. This gives you the ability to add additional logic (like validation) to attribute access, while keeping the outside interface clean and simple.
4. **Validation and Logic Handling:**
   - Using properties, you can add logic to check or modify data before it is returned or updated. For instance, in the example above, we added validation to ensure the `age` is always positive before it is set.

This validation could involve complex logic, such as ensuring an email follows a certain format, or checking the range of numerical values.

5. **Supports Abstraction and Flexibility:**
   o Properties allow you to hide the implementation details of how attributes are stored. You can modify the internal implementation (like changing the underlying data type or storage method) without affecting the external interface of the class. This helps maintain a stable API while enabling changes to internal details.
6. **No Change in Interface:**
   o If you need to change the way an attribute is computed or validated, using `@property` makes it easy to do so without changing the way external code accesses or modifies the attribute.

When to Use @property

- **When you need to calculate or modify values dynamically** (e.g., computing the value based on other internal attributes) while still providing a simple attribute-like interface.
- **When you want to enforce validation** before setting an attribute's value, ensuring that only valid data can be assigned.
- **When you want to control access** to an attribute or restrict modification by making certain methods read-only or write-only.
- **When you want to hide the complexity** of an implementation while keeping the interface clean.

5. Real-world Examples of Encapsulation

Encapsulation is a key concept in object-oriented programming (OOP) that involves bundling data and methods that operate on that data into a single unit, typically a class. By restricting direct access to some of the object's components, encapsulation allows you to control how the data is accessed or modified. This concept is widely used in real-world applications to enforce data integrity and abstraction.

Here are detailed explanations of real-world scenarios where encapsulation is used:

Example 1: Bank Account System

In a banking system, encapsulation helps prevent unauthorized or invalid operations on an account's sensitive data, such as the balance. By using private attributes and controlled access through methods, the integrity of the account is maintained.

Implementation:

```python
class BankAccount:
    def __init__(self, balance):
        self.__balance = balance  # Private attribute to store account balance

    # Getter for balance
    @property
    def balance(self):
        return self.__balance

    # Setter for balance with validation
    @balance.setter
    def balance(self, amount):
        if amount >= 0:
            self.__balance = amount
        else:
            print("Balance cannot be negative.")

    # Method to deposit money
    def deposit(self, amount):
        if amount > 0:
            self.__balance += amount
        else:
            print("Deposit amount should be positive.")

    # Method to withdraw money
    def withdraw(self, amount):
        if amount <= self.__balance:
            self.__balance -= amount
        else:
            print("Insufficient funds.")
```

Usage:

```python
# Creating a bank account with an initial balance
account = BankAccount(1000)

# Accessing the balance via the getter
print(account.balance)   # Output: 1000

# Modifying the balance via the setter
account.balance = 1200
print(account.balance)   # Output: 1200

# Depositing money
account.deposit(500)
```

```
print(account.balance)    # Output: 1700

# Attempting to withdraw more money than the balance
account.withdraw(2000)    # Output: Insufficient funds.

# Withdrawing money within the balance
account.withdraw(700)
print(account.balance)    # Output: 1000
```

Key Benefits in This Example:

- The `__balance` attribute is private, ensuring it cannot be directly accessed or modified from outside the class.
- Controlled methods (`deposit, withdraw, balance.setter`) ensure only valid operations are performed.
- Encapsulation prevents accidental or malicious changes to the account balance.

Example 2: Employee Salary Management

In an employee salary management system, encapsulation helps to hide sensitive information like the employee's salary. Only authorized changes are allowed, and validation can be added to ensure data integrity.

Implementation:

```
class Employee:
    def __init__(self, name, salary):
        self.__name = name   # Private attribute for the name
        self.__salary = salary   # Private attribute for the salary

    # Getter for salary
    @property
    def salary(self):
        return self.__salary

    # Setter for salary with validation
    @salary.setter
    def salary(self, new_salary):
        if new_salary >= 0:
            self.__salary = new_salary
        else:
            print("Salary cannot be negative.")

    # Method to display employee details
    def display_info(self):
        print(f"Employee: {self.__name}, Salary: {self.__salary}")
```

Usage:

```
# Creating an employee object
```

```
employee = Employee("John", 50000)

# Displaying initial employee information
employee.display_info()   # Output: Employee: John, Salary: 50000

# Modifying the salary via the setter
employee.salary = 55000
employee.display_info()   # Output: Employee: John, Salary: 55000

# Attempting to set an invalid salary
employee.salary = -10000  # Output: Salary cannot be negative.
```

Key Benefits in This Example:

- The __salary attribute is private, ensuring that it cannot be directly modified.
- The setter ensures that invalid salary values (e.g., negative numbers) are rejected.
- Encapsulation hides the internal representation of salary while providing controlled access through getter and setter methods.

Why Encapsulation is Important in Real-world Scenarios

1. **Data Security and Integrity:**
   o Encapsulation ensures sensitive data (like bank balances or employee salaries) cannot be accidentally or maliciously altered.
2. **Abstraction:**
   o It hides the internal implementation details from the user, allowing them to interact with only the necessary parts of the system.
3. **Validation and Control:**
   o By using getter and setter methods, you can add validation logic to ensure only valid data is processed.
4. **Modularity:**
   o Encapsulation helps organize code into logical sections, making it easier to maintain and debug.
5. **Reusability:**
   o Encapsulation makes it easier to reuse code in different parts of the application since the implementation details are hidden.

Other Real-world Examples of Encapsulation

1. **Online Shopping Systems:**
   o Encapsulation can manage sensitive customer data (e.g., payment details, address) and ensure access is controlled via methods.
2. **Healthcare Systems:**
   o Patient data, such as medical history, prescriptions, and diagnoses, is encapsulated to prevent unauthorized access.

3. **Gaming Applications:**
   - o Player statistics (e.g., health points, level, score) are encapsulated to ensure they can only be modified through specific methods, preventing cheating or errors.
4. **IoT Devices:**
   - o Smart devices encapsulate settings and data (e.g., temperature in a thermostat), allowing controlled access and updates through methods or APIs.

MCQ

1. Understanding Encapsulation

Q1: What is encapsulation in object-oriented programming?
a) Binding variables and functions together in a class
b) Hiding implementation details while exposing essential functionalities
c) Both a and b
d) None of the above
Answer: c

Q2: Encapsulation ensures:
a) Code modularity
b) Data security
c) Data hiding
d) All of the above
Answer: d

Q3: Which concept is achieved using encapsulation?
a) Abstraction
b) Polymorphism
c) Inheritance
d) Both a and b
Answer: a

Q4: Encapsulation primarily works with:
a) Classes and objects
b) Functions and variables
c) Modules and libraries
d) Statements and conditions
Answer: a

Q5: Which is NOT a benefit of encapsulation?
a) Better code readability
b) Unrestricted access to private data
c) Enhanced security

d) Controlled access to attributes
Answer: b

---

2. Private and Public Attributes

Q6: How do you define a private attribute in Python?
a) Using a single underscore (_) prefix
b) Using a double underscore (__) prefix
c) Using a dollar sign ($) prefix
d) By making the attribute name uppercase
Answer: b

Q7: Which of the following is a public attribute?
a) `_attribute`
b) `__attribute`
c) `attribute`
d) None of the above
Answer: c

Q8: What happens if you try to access a private attribute directly?
a) The program throws a runtime error
b) Python raises an AttributeError
c) The program executes without any issue
d) Python automatically makes it public
Answer: b

Q9: How can you access a private attribute in Python indirectly?
a) By creating a direct object reference
b) Using getter and setter methods
c) By redefining the attribute as public
d) Using the `private` keyword
Answer: b

Q10: What is the naming convention for private attributes?
a) `__attribute`
b) `_attribute`
c) `attribute`
d) Both a and b
Answer: d

3. Getter and Setter Methods

Q11: What is the purpose of a getter method in Python?
a) To modify the value of an attribute
b) To retrieve the value of an attribute
c) To delete an attribute
d) None of the above
Answer: b

Q12: Which of the following statements is true about setter methods?
a) They are used to retrieve private attribute values.
b) They are used to modify private attribute values.
c) They can only be used with public attributes.
d) They do not allow validation logic.
Answer: b

Q13: Why should you use getter and setter methods instead of directly accessing attributes?
a) To hide implementation details
b) To add validation logic
c) To improve code maintainability
d) All of the above
Answer: d

Q14: Which of the following is a correct implementation of a setter method?

```
class Example:
    def __init__(self, value):
        self.__value = value

    def set_value(self, value):
        self.__value = value
```

a) Correct implementation
b) Incorrect implementation due to missing validation
c) Incorrect implementation due to syntax error
d) None of the above
Answer: b

Q15: What will happen if a setter method does not include validation?
a) It ensures strict control of the attribute.
b) It allows potentially invalid values to be set.
c) It prevents attribute modification.
d) It raises a runtime error.
Answer: b

4. Using @property Decorator

Q16: What does the `@property` decorator do?
a) Makes a method private
b) Converts a method into a getter
c) Converts a method into a setter
d) None of the above
Answer: b

Q17: Which of the following is required to define a setter method using the `@property` decorator?
a) `@property`
b) `@method_name.setter`
c) `@method_name.getter`
d) Both a and b
Answer: d

Q18: In the following code, which attribute does the setter method modify?

```
class Example:
    def __init__(self):
        self.__value = 0

    @property
    def value(self):
        return self.__value

    @value.setter
    def value(self, val):
        self.__value = val
```

a) `__value`
b) `value`
c) Both `__value` and `value`
d) None of the above
Answer: a

Q19: What will the following code output?

```
class Test:
    def __init__(self, val):
        self.__val = val

    @property
    def val(self):
        return self.__val

    @val.setter
    def val(self, val):
        self.__val = val
```

```
obj = Test(10)
print(obj.val)
```

a) 10
b) __val
c) Error: Private attribute access
d) None of the above
Answer: a

Q20: Which of the following is a key benefit of using `@property`?
a) Avoiding redundant getter and setter method calls
b) Direct access to private attributes
c) Faster execution
d) None of the above
Answer: a

Mixed Questions

Q21: Which Python feature makes encapsulation more elegant?
a) `@staticmethod`
b) `@classmethod`
c) `@property`
d) `@abstractmethod`
Answer: c

Q22: What is the primary purpose of encapsulation in real-world systems?
a) Simplify algorithms
b) Protect sensitive data
c) Minimize memory usage
d) Avoid loops in code
Answer: b

Q23: Encapsulation can enforce validation by:
a) Using private attributes and exposing them through setter methods
b) Allowing unrestricted access to variables
c) Using only public attributes
d) All of the above
Answer: a

Q24: How does `@property` improve code readability?
a) By allowing attribute-like access to private data
b) By reducing the number of lines in a program
c) By creating immutable objects

```
```

d) None of the above
Answer: a

Q25: In which situation is encapsulation most useful?
a) When implementing class hierarchies
b) When working with large datasets
c) When you need to restrict or validate attribute access
d) When writing standalone functions
Answer: c

Summary:

- **Encapsulation** helps protect the internal state of an object and provides controlled access to its data.
- **Private and public attributes** define the level of accessibility to data.
- **Getter and setter methods** allow you to access or modify private attributes safely.
- **@property decorators** simplify getter and setter implementation while providing cleaner code.
- **Real-world examples** show how encapsulation is used in practical applications such as banking and salary management systems.

Encapsulation ensures that the class's internal workings remain hidden from the outside world, making the code more secure, maintainable, and easier to manage.

CHAPTER 4: INHERITANCE

1. What is Inheritance?

Inheritance is a fundamental concept in object-oriented programming (OOP) that allows one class (child or derived class) to inherit attributes and methods from another class (parent or base class). It promotes code reuse and establishes a hierarchy between classes.

- **Key Benefits of Inheritance**:
    - Code Reusability: Allows a child class to reuse the parent class's methods and attributes.
    - Modularity: Separates functionality into hierarchical structures.
    - Extensibility: Facilitates adding new functionalities to existing classes without modifying them.
    - Polymorphism: Supports method overriding for specialized behavior.

Example of Inheritance in the Real World: A base class `Vehicle` can have attributes like `speed` and `fuel`. Derived classes like `Car` and `Bike` can inherit these attributes and methods while adding their specific properties, such as `number_of_doors` for `Car`.

---

2. Implementing Inheritance in Python

Python supports inheritance through the syntax `class ChildClass(ParentClass)`. Here's how it works:

```python
# Base Class
class Animal:
    def __init__(self, name):
        self.name = name

    def speak(self):
        return f"{self.name} makes a sound."

# Derived Class
class Dog(Animal):
    def speak(self):
        return f"{self.name} barks."

# Usage
dog = Dog("Buddy")
print(dog.speak())   # Output: Buddy barks.
```

Key Points:

- The `Dog` class inherits the `__init__` method from `Animal` but overrides the `speak` method.

- Inheritance is indicated by placing the parent class name in parentheses after the child class name.

---

3. Types of Inheritance in Python

Inheritance allows classes to reuse and extend the functionality of existing classes. Python supports the following types of inheritance:

---

1. Single Inheritance

In single inheritance, a child class inherits from only one parent class. It is the simplest form of inheritance.

- **Usage**: When there is a straightforward relationship between two classes.

Example:

```
class Parent:
    def greet(self):
        print("Hello from Parent.")

class Child(Parent):
    def display(self):
        print("This is the Child class.")

# Usage
child = Child()
child.greet()    # Output: Hello from Parent.
child.display()  # Output: This is the Child class.
```

---

2. Multiple Inheritance

In multiple inheritance, a child class inherits from two or more parent classes. This can lead to ambiguity if both parent classes have methods with the same name (resolved using Method Resolution Order or MRO).

- **Usage**: When a class needs to combine functionalities of multiple parent classes.

Example:

```
class Father:
    def skill(self):
        print("Father: Driving.")
```

```
class Mother:
    def skill(self):
        print("Mother: Cooking.")

class Child(Father, Mother):
    pass

# Usage
child = Child()
child.skill()  # Output: Father: Driving. (Based on MRO)
```

Key Point:

- The method from the first-listed parent class (Father) is used due to Python's MRO.

---

3. Multilevel Inheritance

In multilevel inheritance, a class inherits from another class, which in turn inherits from a third class, forming a chain.

- **Usage**: When there is a hierarchy or progression in relationships between classes.

Example:

```
class Grandparent:
    def legacy(self):
        print("Grandparent: Inheritance of wisdom.")

class Parent(Grandparent):
    def tradition(self):
        print("Parent: Continuing traditions.")

class Child(Parent):
    def innovation(self):
        print("Child: Adding innovation.")

# Usage
child = Child()
child.legacy()  # Output: Grandparent: Inheritance of wisdom.
child.tradition()  # Output: Parent: Continuing traditions.
child.innovation()  # Output: Child: Adding innovation.
```

---

4. Hierarchical Inheritance

In hierarchical inheritance, multiple child classes inherit from a single parent class. Each child class has access to the methods and attributes of the parent class.

- **Usage**: When several classes share common behavior provided by a single parent class.

Example:

```
class Animal:
    def speak(self):
        print("Animal makes a sound.")

class Dog(Animal):
    def speak(self):
        print("Dog barks.")

class Cat(Animal):
    def speak(self):
        print("Cat meows.")

# Usage
dog = Dog()
cat = Cat()
dog.speak()   # Output: Dog barks.
cat.speak()   # Output: Cat meows.
```

5. Hybrid Inheritance

Hybrid inheritance is a combination of two or more types of inheritance. It can involve single, multiple, hierarchical, or multilevel inheritance.

- **Usage**: In complex systems where multiple types of inheritance are needed.

Example:

```
class Animal:
    def speak(self):
        print("Animal speaks.")

class Mammal(Animal):
    def walk(self):
        print("Mammal walks.")

class Bird(Animal):
    def fly(self):
        print("Bird flies.")

class Bat(Mammal, Bird):
    pass

# Usage
bat = Bat()
bat.speak()   # Output: Animal speaks.
bat.walk()    # Output: Mammal walks.
```

```
bat.fly()   # Output: Bird flies.
```

Key Point:

- Python uses MRO to resolve method calls in hybrid inheritance, ensuring no ambiguity.

6. Multiple Levels of Combination in Hybrid

When combining types of inheritance, Python handles ambiguities using the **C3 Linearization Algorithm** to create a specific order of method resolution.

4. Method Overriding

Definition:
Method overriding occurs when a derived (child) class provides its specific implementation for a method that is already defined in its parent class. The overridden method in the child class must have the **same name, parameters, and return type** as the method in the parent class.

Purpose of Method Overriding

- To **customize** or **extend** the behavior of a method inherited from the parent class.
- To provide a **specialized implementation** in the child class while retaining the general structure of the parent class.
- To achieve **polymorphism**, where the behavior of the method depends on the object type at runtime.

Key Characteristics of Method Overriding

1. **Same Method Signature**:
   - The method in the child class must have the same name and parameters as the method in the parent class.
2. **Precedence**:
   - The method in the child class takes precedence over the parent class method when called on a child class object.
3. **Polymorphism**:

- o Overriding supports polymorphism, allowing the program to decide at runtime which method to invoke based on the object's type.
4. **Optional Call to Parent's Method**:
    - o You can still access the overridden method in the parent class using the `super()` function.

Basic Example of Method Overriding

```
class Parent:
    def greet(self):
        print("Hello from Parent.")

class Child(Parent):
    def greet(self):
        print("Hello from Child.")

# Usage
obj = Child()
obj.greet()   # Output: Hello from Child.
```

Explanation:
The `greet()` method in the `Child` class overrides the `greet()` method in the `Parent` class. When called on a `Child` object, the overridden method in `Child` is executed.

Accessing the Parent's Method Using `super()`

Sometimes, the child class might want to add to the behavior of the parent method instead of completely replacing it.

Example:

```
:
    def greet(self):
        print("Hello from Parent.")

class Child(Parent):
    def greet(self):
        super().greet()   # Call the parent class method
        print("Hello from Child.")

# Usage
obj = Child()
obj.greet()
```

Output:

```
Hello from Parent.
Hello from Child.
```

Explanation:
The `super().greet()` call executes the parent class's method, and then the child class adds its additional behavior.

Practical Example: Employee and Manager

```python
class Employee:
    def work(self):
        print("Employee: Completing assigned tasks.")

class Manager(Employee):
    def work(self):
        print("Manager: Assigning tasks to employees.")

# Usage
e = Employee()
e.work()   # Output: Employee: Completing assigned tasks.

m = Manager()
m.work()   # Output: Manager: Assigning tasks to employees.
```

Explanation:
The `Manager` class overrides the `work()` method to reflect its specialized responsibilities.

Method Overriding and Polymorphism

Polymorphism occurs when the overridden method is called dynamically based on the object type at runtime.

Example:

```python
class Animal:
    def speak(self):
        print("Animal makes a sound.")

class Dog(Animal):
    def speak(self):
        print("Dog barks.")

class Cat(Animal):
    def speak(self):
        print("Cat meows.")
```

```
# Usage
animals = [Dog(), Cat()]

for animal in animals:
    animal.speak()
```

Output:

```
Cat meows.
```

Explanation:
Even though `animals` is a list of `Animal` objects, the `speak()` method of the specific subclass (`Dog` or `Cat`) is executed, demonstrating polymorphism.

Rules of Method Overriding

1. **Method Name and Signature**:
   o The method name and parameter list in the child class must match the method in the parent class.
2. **Inheritance**:
   o Method overriding is only possible if there is an inheritance relationship between the parent and child classes.
3. **Access Modifiers**:
   o The access level of the overridden method in the child class should not be more restrictive than that of the parent class method.

Advantages of Method Overriding

1. **Code Reusability**:
   o The child class reuses the method definition of the parent class, modifying only the necessary parts.
2. **Custom Behavior**:
   o Allows classes to implement custom behavior specific to their context.
3. **Runtime Polymorphism**:
   o Enables dynamic method dispatch, which is fundamental in object-oriented design.

5. The `super()` Function

The `super()` function in Python is a built-in utility used to access methods and attributes of the parent class from within a child class. It is primarily used to **call parent class methods or constructors** to ensure the base functionality is preserved while extending or customizing it in the child class.

Why Use `super()`?

1. **Eliminates Explicit Parent Class Name**:
   Using `super()` avoids hardcoding the parent class name, which makes the code more maintainable, especially in case of class name changes.
2. **Supports Multiple Inheritance**:
   It ensures proper resolution of methods in the inheritance hierarchy using the **Method Resolution Order (MRO)**.
3. **Extends Parent Class Functionality**:
   It allows the child class to reuse parent class methods while adding or overriding specific behaviors.

Basic Syntax

```
super().method_name(arguments)
```

Example 1: Calling Parent Class Constructor

```
class Parent:
    def __init__(self, name):
        self.name = name

class Child(Parent):
    def __init__(self, name, age):
        super().__init__(name)  # Call Parent's constructor
        self.age = age

# Usage
obj = Child("Alice", 12)
print(f"Name: {obj.name}, Age: {obj.age}")
```

Output:

```
Name: Alice, Age: 12
```

Explanation:

The `super().__init__(name)` call invokes the `__init__` method of the `Parent` class, initializing the `name` attribute. The `Child` class constructor then adds the `age` attribute.

Example 2: Extending Parent Class Methods

```
class Parent:
    def greet(self):
        print("Hello from Parent.")

class Child(Parent):
    def greet(self):
        super().greet()   # Call Parent's greet
        print("Hello from Child.")

# Usage
obj = Child()
obj.greet()
```

Output:

```
Hello from Parent.
Hello from Child.
```

Explanation:

The `super().greet()` call invokes the `greet` method of the `Parent` class before executing the additional code in the `Child` class's `greet` method.

Key Features of `super()`

1. **Dynamic Parent Class Resolution**:
   o `super()` dynamically determines the parent class based on the MRO.
   o This is especially important in multiple inheritance scenarios.
2. **Avoids Hardcoding Class Names**:
   o Using `super()` improves code maintainability by avoiding explicit references to the parent class name.
3. **Ensures MRO Compliance**:
   o In multiple inheritance, `super()` follows the MRO, ensuring that the correct parent method is called.

Method Resolution Order (MRO)

MRO determines the sequence in which classes are searched for methods or attributes when using `super()`. The `mro()` method of a class can be used to inspect the order.

Example:

```
class A:
    def greet(self):
        print("Hello from A.")

class B(A):
    def greet(self):
        print("Hello from B.")
        super().greet()

class C(A):
    def greet(self):
        print("Hello from C.")
        super().greet()

class D(B, C):
    def greet(self):
        print("Hello from D.")
        super().greet()

# Usage
obj = D()
obj.greet()
print(D.mro())
```

Output:

```
Hello from D.
Hello from B.
Hello from C.
Hello from A.
[<class '__main__.D'>, <class '__main__.B'>, <class '__main__.C'>,
<class '__main__.A'>, <class 'object'>]
```

Explanation:
The MRO ensures that methods are called in the order [D, B, C, A, object]. This prevents redundant calls and maintains consistency.

Example 3: Multiple Inheritance

```
class Base1:
    def greet(self):
        print("Hello from Base1.")
```

```
class Base2:
    def greet(self):
        print("Hello from Base2.")

class Derived(Base1, Base2):
    def greet(self):
        super().greet()  # Resolves using MRO

# Usage
obj = Derived()
obj.greet()
print(Derived.mro())
```

Output:

```
Hello from Base1.
[<class '__main__.Derived'>, <class '__main__.Base1'>, <class
'__main__.Base2'>, <class 'object'>]
```

Explanation:
The MRO determines that `Base1.greet()` is called before `Base2.greet()` due to the order of inheritance.

Practical Applications of `super()`

1. **Extending Initialization**:
   A child class can add its attributes while ensuring the parent class's attributes are properly initialized.
2. **Accessing Overridden Methods**:
   Child classes can call methods from the parent class even if they override them.
3. **Resolving Ambiguities in Multiple Inheritance**:
   Using `super()` ensures that methods are called in the correct order according to MRO.

Common Pitfalls

1. **Calling Without Parent Method**:
   If the parent class does not define the method, `super()` will raise an error.
2. **Incorrect Argument Passing**:
   Ensure arguments passed to `super()` match the parent class method's signature.
3. **Not Understanding MRO**:
   In complex inheritance hierarchies, the behavior of `super()` might seem counterintuitive without understanding MRO.

Summary of Key Points

- `super()` is used to call methods or constructors of the parent class.
- It eliminates the need to explicitly reference the parent class name.
- It supports multiple inheritance and adheres to the MRO.
- Useful for extending or modifying parent class behavior in child classes.

6. Practical Applications

Inheritance is extensively used in real-world programming for creating structured and modular applications.

1. **User Roles in Systems**:
   - **Base Class**: User with attributes like name and email.
   - **Derived Classes**: Admin, Guest, and Member can inherit from User and have specific attributes or methods.

```
class User:
    def __init__(self, name, email):
        self.name = name
        self.email = email

class Admin(User):
    def access_panel(self):
        print(f"{self.name} has admin access.")

admin = Admin("John", "john@example.com")
admin.access_panel()  # Output: John has admin access.
```

2. **Game Development**:
   - **Base Class**: Character with attributes like health and speed.
   - **Derived Classes**: Player, Enemy, and NPC can inherit and specialize the base behavior.
3. **E-Commerce Applications**:
   - **Base Class**: Product with attributes like name and price.
   - **Derived Classes**: Electronic, Clothing, and Grocery can extend with their specific features.
4. **Shapes in Graphics**:
   - **Base Class**: Shape with methods like draw().
   - **Derived Classes**: Circle, Rectangle, and Triangle with specialized drawing methods.

MCQ

1. What is the purpose of inheritance in Python?

A. To define functions
B. To reuse code from a parent class
C. To restrict access to class methods
D. To create immutable classes

Answer: B

---

2. Inheritance allows which of the following?

A. Encapsulation
B. Code duplication
C. Code reusability
D. Syntax errors

Answer: C

---

3. What is a child class?

A. A class that inherits from another class
B. A class that has no attributes
C. A class that cannot be instantiated
D. A class with only private methods

Answer: A

---

4. Which keyword is used to inherit a parent class in Python?

A. extends
B. inherits
C. class
D. None of the above

Answer: C

5. What happens if the child class does not override a method in the parent class?

A. The program will crash
B. The parent class method is called by default
C. The method becomes undefined
D. Python raises a runtime error

Answer: B

---

6. How can you access the parent class method in a child class?

A. Using `super()`
B. Using the parent class name
C. Both A and B
D. None of the above

Answer: C

---

7. Which method in Python initializes the attributes of a class?

A. `__new__()`
B. `__str__()`
C. `__init__()`
D. `__del__()`

Answer: C

---

8. In single inheritance, how many parent classes can a child class have?

A. One
B. Two
C. Unlimited
D. None

Answer: A

---

9. What does the `super()` function do?

A. Calls the child class method
B. Calls the parent class method
C. Deletes attributes of the child class
D. None of the above

Answer: B

10. What is the Method Resolution Order (MRO)?

A. The order in which methods are called from the child class
B. The order in which parent classes are searched for a method
C. The order in which attributes are deleted
D. None of the above

Answer: B

11. What is multiple inheritance?

A. A class inheriting multiple attributes
B. A class inheriting from multiple parent classes
C. A class with multiple methods
D. None of the above

Answer: B

12. Which of these scenarios benefits most from inheritance?

A. Defining an unrelated class
B. Sharing common behavior between related classes
C. Writing independent methods
D. None of the above

Answer: B

13. If a class B inherits from class A, how do you specify this in Python?

A. `class B.inherits(A):`
B. `class B.extends(A):`
C. `class B(A):`
D. None of the above

Answer: C

---

14. What is method overriding?

A. Overwriting the parent class method in a child class
B. Copying the parent class method in the child class
C. Using the parent class method without changes
D. None of the above

Answer: A

---

15. Can a child class override the parent class constructor (__init__)?

A. Yes
B. No
C. Only in single inheritance
D. Only in multiple inheritance

Answer: A

---

16. Which of the following is true about the `super()` function?

A. It is used to access methods of the child class
B. It supports multiple inheritance
C. It skips the Method Resolution Order (MRO)
D. None of the above

Answer: B

17. Which of these is an example of single inheritance?

A. `class A: pass; class B: pass; class C(B, A): pass`
B. `class A: pass; class B(A): pass`
C. `class A(B): pass; class B(A): pass`
D. None of the above

Answer: B

---

18. Which error is raised if a parent class method is not found during inheritance?

A. AttributeError
B. NameError
C. TypeError
D. None of the above

Answer: A

---

19. How do you call a parent class method explicitly?

A. `Parent.method()`
B. `super.method()`
C. Both A and B
D. None of the above

Answer: C

---

20. Can a child class inherit private attributes from the parent class?

A. Yes
B. No
C. Only with `super()`
D. None of the above

Answer: B

21. In multiple inheritance, if both parent classes have a method with the same name, which method is called?

A. The method of the first parent class in MRO
B. The method of the second parent class in MRO
C. The method of the child class
D. None of the above

Answer: A

---

22. Which decorator is used for defining properties in a class?

A. `@staticmethod`
B. `@property`
C. `@classmethod`
D. None of the above

Answer: B

---

23. Can a child class add new methods to its parent class?

A. Yes, only using `super()`
B. No, it cannot
C. Yes, independently in the child class
D. None of the above

Answer: C

---

24. What happens if `super()` is not used in the child class constructor?

A. Parent class attributes may not be initialized
B. Parent class methods will not work
C. Both A and B
D. None of the above

Answer: A

---

25. How does Python resolve method calls in the presence of multiple inheritance?

A. Based on alphabetical order of classes
B. Using the Method Resolution Order (MRO)
C. By the class that was defined last
D. None of the above

Answer: B

Summary

Inheritance in Python is a powerful mechanism to reuse and extend existing code. Concepts like single and multiple inheritance, method overriding, and the `super()` function provide flexibility and control. Practical applications of inheritance make it indispensable for developing scalable and maintainable software systems.

CHAPTER 5: POLYMORPHISM

Polymorphism in Python allows objects of different classes to be treated as objects of a common super class. It provides a way to perform a single action in different forms, enabling flexibility and extensibility in code. Let's explore the key topics in detail:

1. Understanding Polymorphism

Definition: Polymorphism is the ability of an object to take on multiple forms. It allows the same interface to be used for different underlying data types.

- **Types of Polymorphism**:
    - **Compile-time Polymorphism**: Achieved using method overloading (not natively supported in Python).
    - **Run-time Polymorphism**: Achieved through method overriding.
- **Example**: Polymorphism with a common method in unrelated classes:

```
class Dog:
    def speak(self):
        return "Woof!"

class Cat:
    def speak(self):
        return "Meow!"

def animal_sound(animal):
    print(animal.speak())

dog = Dog()
cat = Cat()
animal_sound(dog)    # Output: Woof!
animal_sound(cat)    # Output: Meow!
```

Key Advantages:

- Reduces complexity by allowing the same operation on different data types.
- Promotes code reusability and flexibility.

2. Method Overloading (Not Directly Supported in Python)

What is Method Overloading?

Method overloading allows defining multiple methods with the same name but different parameter lists. Depending on the number or types of arguments passed to the method, the appropriate method is executed. This is commonly used in statically typed languages like Java and C++.

Does Python Support Method Overloading?

Python **does not natively support method overloading**. In Python:

- A method in a class can only have **one definition**. If you define a method with the same name multiple times, the most recent definition will overwrite the previous ones.
- However, you can **simulate method overloading** using techniques like:
  - **Default arguments**
  - **Variable-length arguments** (`*args` and `**kwargs`)

Simulating Method Overloading in Python

1. Using Default Arguments

Default arguments allow you to define a single method that can handle multiple scenarios by assigning default values to parameters.

Example:

```python
class Calculator:
    def add(self, a, b=0, c=0):  # Default values for b and c
        return a + b + c

calc = Calculator()
print(calc.add(5))          # Output: 5 (only 'a' is provided; b and c default to 0)
print(calc.add(5, 10))      # Output: 15 (only 'a' and 'b' are provided; c defaults to 0)
print(calc.add(5, 10, 15))  # Output: 30 (all three arguments are provided)
```

Key Points:

- The method is defined only once.
- Default arguments provide flexibility for different numbers of arguments without creating separate methods.

---

2. Using Variable-Length Arguments (*args and **kwargs)

*args and **kwargs allow methods to accept a variable number of positional or keyword arguments, enabling a dynamic approach to method overloading.

Example: Using *args for Positional Arguments

```
class Calculator:
    def add(self, *args):  # Accepts any number of positional arguments
        return sum(args)

calc = Calculator()
print(calc.add(5))           # Output: 5
print(calc.add(5, 10))       # Output: 15
print(calc.add(5, 10, 15))   # Output: 30
```

Explanation:

- The *args syntax collects all provided arguments into a tuple.
- You can iterate over the arguments or use functions like sum() to perform operations.

Example: Using **kwargs for Keyword Arguments

```
class Calculator:
    def add(self, **kwargs):  # Accepts any number of keyword arguments
        return sum(kwargs.values())

calc = Calculator()
print(calc.add(a=5))            # Output: 5
print(calc.add(a=5, b=10))      # Output: 15
print(calc.add(a=5, b=10, c=15)) # Output: 30
```

Explanation:

- The **kwargs syntax collects all provided keyword arguments into a dictionary.
- You can access the values of the dictionary to perform operations.

3. Method Dispatch Based on Argument Types

To simulate method overloading based on argument types, you can use conditional checks inside a method.

Example:

```python
class Calculator:
    def add(self, a, b=None):
        if b is None:  # Single argument case
            return a
        elif isinstance(a, str) and isinstance(b, str):  # Both
arguments are strings
            return a + b
        else:  # Both arguments are numbers
            return a + b

calc = Calculator()
print(calc.add(5))             # Output: 5 (single argument)
print(calc.add(5, 10))         # Output: 15 (both arguments are numbers)
print(calc.add("Hello, ", "World!"))  # Output: Hello, World! (both
arguments are strings)
```

Limitations of Method Overloading in Python

- Python does not perform compile-time checks for method signatures, unlike statically typed languages.
- There is no direct support for method overloading; instead, you must use workarounds like default arguments or dynamic argument handling.

Summary

Technique	Description	Example Usage
Default Arguments	Provides default values for parameters.	Handling different numbers of arguments.
Variable-Length Args	Uses `*args` or `**kwargs` to accept any number of arguments.	Flexible and dynamic argument handling.
Type-based Dispatch	Uses `if` or `isinstance()` to vary behavior based on argument type.	Simulates type-based overloading.

Although Python lacks native method overloading, its dynamic nature and flexible function signatures enable powerful workarounds. These techniques make Python's approach to overloading more practical and adaptable for real-world programming.

3. Method Overriding with Examples

What is Method Overriding?

Method overriding occurs when:

- A **child class** defines a method with the same name, signature, and return type as a method in its **parent class**.
- The method in the **child class takes precedence** over the method in the parent class when invoked using an instance of the child class.

Key Points:

1. **Purpose:**
   - Method overriding is used to **specialize** or **modify behavior** in the child class while reusing the functionality of the parent class.
2. **Polymorphism:**
   - It enables **run-time polymorphism**, where the type of the object determines which version of the method is executed.
3. **super() Function:**
   - The `super()` function allows the child class to invoke the parent class's method. This is useful for extending the functionality of the parent method instead of completely replacing it.

Examples of Method Overriding

1. Basic Method Overriding

In this example, the child class provides a specialized implementation of the `show_message` method.

```
class Parent:
    def show_message(self):
        print("Message from Parent")

class Child(Parent):
    def show_message(self):
        print("Message from Child")

# Create an instance of Child and call the overridden method
obj = Child()
obj.show_message()
```

Output:

```
Message from Child
```

Explanation:

- The `show_message` method in the **Child** class overrides the method in the **Parent** class.
- When `obj.show_message()` is called, the **Child's** version of the method is executed.

---

2. Using `super()` to Call the Parent Class Method

By using `super()`, the child class can invoke the parent class method and add additional functionality.

```python
class Parent:
    def show_message(self):
        print("Message from Parent")

class Child(Parent):
    def show_message(self):
        super().show_message()  # Call Parent's method
        print("Message from Child")  # Add additional functionality

# Create an instance of Child and call the overridden method
obj = Child()
obj.show_message()
```

Output:

```
Message from Parent
Message from Child
```

Explanation:

- `super().show_message()` calls the `show_message` method of the **Parent** class.
- The `Child` class then adds its own behavior after executing the parent's method.

---

3. Overriding with Additional Parameters

A child class can define a method with additional parameters while still overriding the parent's method.

```python
class Parent:
    def show_message(self):
        print("Message from Parent")
```

```
class Child(Parent):
    def show_message(self, additional_message):
        print("Message from Child")
        print(f"Additional Message: {additional_message}")

# Create an instance of Child and call the overridden method
obj = Child()
obj.show_message("Hello, Python!")
```

Output:

```
Message from Child
Additional Message: Hello, Python!
```

Explanation:

- The `Child` class overrides the parent's `show_message` method by accepting an additional parameter.

---

4. Overriding in a Hierarchical Structure

Overriding works consistently in a multi-level inheritance hierarchy.

```
class Grandparent:
    def show_message(self):
        print("Message from Grandparent")

class Parent(Grandparent):
    def show_message(self):
        print("Message from Parent")

class Child(Parent):
    def show_message(self):
        super().show_message()  # Call Parent's method
        print("Message from Child")

# Create an instance of Child and call the overridden method
obj = Child()
obj.show_message()
```

Output:

```
Message from Parent
Message from Child
```

Explanation:

- `super().show_message()` in the `Child` class calls the method in the **Parent** class, not the **Grandparent** class.

- This is due to Python's **Method Resolution Order (MRO)**.

Polymorphism with Method Overriding

Method overriding enables polymorphism by allowing a child class to define its own behavior while sharing a common interface with the parent class.

Example:

```
class Animal:
    def make_sound(self):
        print("Some generic sound")

class Dog(Animal):
    def make_sound(self):
        print("Bark")

class Cat(Animal):
    def make_sound(self):
        print("Meow")

# Polymorphism: Using the same interface
animals = [Dog(), Cat(), Animal()]

for animal in animals:
    animal.make_sound()
```

Output:

```
Bark
Meow
Some generic sound
```

Explanation:

- The make_sound method is overridden in the Dog and Cat classes.
- The method call is resolved based on the type of the object at runtime.

Best Practices for Method Overriding

1. Use **super()** to ensure that the parent class's functionality is not lost if needed.
2. Clearly document the overridden methods to avoid confusion.
3. Maintain consistency in method signatures unless additional parameters are absolutely necessary.

Summary Table

Feature	Method Overriding
Definition	Redefining a method in the child class that already exists in the parent class.
Purpose	To provide specialized behavior in the child class.
Polymorphism	Supports run-time polymorphism, enabling different behaviors based on the object type.
Key Function	Use `super()` to invoke the parent class method while overriding.
Example Scenario	Animal hierarchy (e.g., `Dog` and `Cat` overriding `make_sound` from `Animal`).

Method overriding is a powerful feature of object-oriented programming in Python that promotes code reusability, modularity, and flexibility.

---

4. Using Polymorphism in Real-world Scenarios

Polymorphism is widely used in various real-world scenarios, such as:

Example 1: File Operations Different file types may implement a common interface to perform operations like `read` and `write`.

```
class TextFile:
    def open(self):
        print("Opening text file...")

class ImageFile:
    def open(self):
        print("Opening image file...")

def open_file(file):
    file.open()

txt = TextFile()
img = ImageFile()
open_file(txt)   # Output: Opening text file...
open_file(img)   # Output: Opening image file...
```

Example 2: Shapes in a Drawing Application Common interface for different shapes:

```
class Shape:
    def draw(self):
        pass
```

```
class Circle(Shape):
    def draw(self):
        print("Drawing a Circle")

class Square(Shape):
    def draw(self):
        print("Drawing a Square")

shapes = [Circle(), Square()]
for shape in shapes:
    shape.draw()
# Output:
# Drawing a Circle
# Drawing a Square
```

Example 3: Dynamic Dispatch in a Payment System Different payment methods (credit card, PayPal) can implement the same interface:

```
class Payment:
    def process_payment(self):
        pass

class CreditCardPayment(Payment):
    def process_payment(self):
        print("Processing credit card payment")

class PayPalPayment(Payment):
    def process_payment(self):
        print("Processing PayPal payment")

def make_payment(payment_method):
    payment_method.process_payment()

cc_payment = CreditCardPayment()
paypal_payment = PayPalPayment()
make_payment(cc_payment)      # Output: Processing credit card payment
make_payment(paypal_payment)  # Output: Processing PayPal payment
```

MCQ

1. Understanding Polymorphism

1. **What is the main idea behind polymorphism in object-oriented programming?**
   - o a) Objects of different classes can share the same method.
   - o b) Objects of the same class can have different methods.
   - o c) A class can have multiple constructors.
   - o d) A method can be inherited by child classes.

   Answer: a) Objects of different classes can share the same method.

2. **Which of the following is true about polymorphism?**
   - o   a) It occurs at compile-time.
   - o   b) It allows methods in different classes to have the same name but behave differently.
   - o   c) It does not support method overriding.
   - o   d) It is limited to method overloading only.

   Answer: b) It allows methods in different classes to have the same name but behave differently.

3. **In which type of polymorphism does the method call depend on the object type at runtime?**
   - o   a) Compile-time polymorphism
   - o   b) Runtime polymorphism
   - o   c) Static polymorphism
   - o   d) Overloading

   Answer: b) Runtime polymorphism

4. **Which of the following best describes polymorphism?**
   - o   a) One method for multiple purposes.
   - o   b) One object for multiple classes.
   - o   c) One class for multiple objects.
   - o   d) Multiple constructors for the same class.

   Answer: a) One method for multiple purposes.

5. **Which principle of OOP allows polymorphism to be achieved?**
   - o   a) Abstraction
   - o   b) Encapsulation
   - o   c) Inheritance
   - o   d) Modularity

   Answer: c) Inheritance

2. Method Overloading (Not Directly Supported in Python)

6. **Which of the following is true about method overloading in Python?**
   - o   a) Python supports method overloading directly.
   - o   b) Python does not support method overloading natively.
   - o   c) Python supports method overloading but requires explicit method definition.
   - o   d) Python uses function overloading to implement polymorphism.

Answer: b) Python does not support method overloading natively.

7. **How can method overloading be simulated in Python?**
    - o a) By defining multiple methods with the same name.
    - o b) By using default arguments or variable-length arguments.
    - o c) By using multiple inheritance.
    - o d) By using `@staticmethod` decorators.

    Answer: b) By using default arguments or variable-length arguments.

8. **Which of the following is an example of method overloading in Python?**
    - o a) Using multiple methods with the same name and different parameters.
    - o b) Using default arguments to modify the behavior of a method.
    - o c) Using the `super()` function.
    - o d) Using `@property` decorators for getter methods.

    Answer: b) Using default arguments to modify the behavior of a method.

9. **What is the primary reason Python does not support method overloading directly?**
    - o a) Python has multiple inheritance.
    - o b) Python uses dynamic typing.
    - o c) Python does not support function overloading in any way.
    - o d) Python's method resolution order is more efficient.

    Answer: b) Python uses dynamic typing.

10. *Which of the following demonstrates simulating method overloading using args?*
    - o a) `def add(a, b): return a + b`
    - o b) `def add(*args): return sum(args)`
    - o c) `def add(a=0, b=0): return a + b`
    - o d) `def add(a, b=0): return a + b`

    Answer: b) `def add(*args): return sum(args)`

---

3. Method Overriding with Examples

11. **What is method overriding?**

- • a) Changing the return type of a method.
- • b) Redefining a method in a child class that already exists in the parent class.
- • c) Adding extra parameters to a method.
- • d) Changing the method's name in the child class.

Answer: b) Redefining a method in a child class that already exists in the parent class.

12. **Which of the following is true about method overriding in Python?**

   - a) The method in the child class must have the same signature as the parent method.
   - b) Method overriding allows the child class to change the method name in the parent class.
   - c) Method overriding results in compile-time errors in Python.
   - d) Method overriding only works with instance variables, not methods.

Answer: a) The method in the child class must have the same signature as the parent method.

13. **Which of the following is a key benefit of method overriding?**

   - a) It helps reuse the parent class code without changes.
   - b) It allows the child class to modify or specialize the behavior of the inherited method.
   - c) It makes the parent class code more complex.
   - d) It forces the parent method to be hidden.

Answer: b) It allows the child class to modify or specialize the behavior of the inherited method.

14. **In Python, which function is used to call the parent class's method inside an overridden method?**

   - a) `super()`
   - b) `parent()`
   - c) `parentClass()`
   - d) `callParent()`

Answer: a) `super()`

15. **Consider the following code. What will be the output?**

```
class Parent:
    def greet(self):
        print("Hello from Parent")

class Child(Parent):
    def greet(self):
        print("Hello from Child")

obj = Child()
obj.greet()
```

   - a) "Hello from Parent"

- b) "Hello from Child"
- c) "Hello from Parent" and "Hello from Child"
- d) Error

Answer: b) "Hello from Child"

16. **What is the purpose of using `super()` in method overriding?**

- a) To override a method in the parent class.
- b) To invoke the method of the parent class from the child class.
- c) To call methods from multiple parent classes.
- d) To hide the parent class method.

Answer: b) To invoke the method of the parent class from the child class.

17. **What will the following code print?**

```
class Parent:
    def display(self):
        print("Parent Display")

class Child(Parent):
    def display(self):
        super().display()
        print("Child Display")

obj = Child()
obj.display()
```

- a) "Child Display"
- b) "Parent Display"
- c) "Parent Display" and "Child Display"
- d) Error

Answer: c) "Parent Display" and "Child Display"

18. **Which of the following types of polymorphism is demonstrated by method overriding?**

- a) Compile-time polymorphism
- b) Runtime polymorphism
- c) Method overloading
- d) None of the above

Answer: b) Runtime polymorphism

19. **In method overriding, if the method in the parent class is not called, what happens?**

- a) The parent class method is always invoked.
- b) The child class method completely replaces the parent class method.
- c) The program raises an exception.
- d) The parent class method runs automatically.

Answer: b) The child class method completely replaces the parent class method.

20. **In the following code, which method will be called when `obj.greet()` is executed?**

```
class A:
    def greet(self):
        print("Hello from A")

class B(A):
    def greet(self):
        print("Hello from B")

obj = B()
obj.greet()
```

- a) greet() from class A
- b) greet() from class B
- c) Both greet() from A and B
- d) None of the above

Answer: b) greet() from class B

General Polymorphism Questions

21. **Which concept allows the same function to behave differently based on the type of object calling it?**

- a) Encapsulation
- b) Inheritance
- c) Polymorphism
- d) Abstraction

Answer: c) Polymorphism

22. **Which of the following is an example of polymorphism in Python?**

- a) A method that can take different numbers of arguments.

- b) A method in the parent class that is overwritten by the child class.
- c) Multiple classes sharing the same method name but implementing it differently.
- d) Both b and c.

Answer: d) Both b and c.

23. **What does the term 'method resolution order' (MRO) refer to in Python?**

- a) The order in which methods are invoked in a class hierarchy.
- b) The order in which methods are defined in a class.
- c) The order in which methods are inherited by subclasses.
- d) The resolution of conflicts in method overloading.

Answer: a) The order in which methods are invoked in a class hierarchy.

24. **What is the result of method overriding in terms of inheritance?**

- a) The child class method takes precedence over the parent class method.
- b) The parent class method is hidden by the child class.
- c) Both the parent and child methods are executed.
- d) The parent class method is executed by default.

Answer: a) The child class method takes precedence over the parent class method.

25. **Which of the following is a feature of runtime polymorphism?**

- a) It is achieved via method overloading.
- b) It is achieved via method overriding.
- c) It is achieved at compile time.
- d) It is implemented through static methods.

Answer: b) It is achieved via method overriding.

Summary of Polymorphism in Python

Feature	Description
Definition	Polymorphism enables performing a single action in multiple ways.
Types	Method Overloading (Compile-time) and Method Overriding (Run-time).
Applications	Code flexibility, reducing duplication, enabling extensibility.

Feature	Description
Real-world Use	File operations, shape drawing, payment systems, and other interface-driven designs.

Polymorphism is a cornerstone of object-oriented programming that brings flexibility and reusability to code while promoting clean and maintainable designs.

CHAPTER 6: ABSTRACTION

1. What is Abstraction?

Abstraction is one of the four fundamental principles of object-oriented programming (OOP), alongside inheritance, encapsulation, and polymorphism. It refers to the concept of hiding the **complexity** of a system and exposing only the necessary details to the user. Abstraction allows us to focus on **what** an object does, rather than **how** it does it.

In simple terms:

- **Abstraction** allows the programmer to define the structure of the system without revealing all the internal workings or implementation details.
- It helps in reducing complexity by providing a simple interface while hiding the implementation details.

Key Points:

- **Hiding Implementation**: Only essential features are exposed, while the internal workings are kept hidden.
- **Simplifying Usage**: It makes interacting with complex systems easier by hiding the unnecessary information.
- **Focus on what is done**: Abstraction allows users to work with concepts and their essential features without needing to understand how they are implemented.

Example:

Consider a **TV Remote Control**:

- **Abstraction**: The remote has buttons like "power", "volume up", "volume down", etc.
- **Hidden Details**: The complex circuitry and processes inside the remote are hidden from the user.

The user is concerned only with the basic functions like changing channels or adjusting volume, while the internal workings are abstracted away.

---

2. Abstract Classes and Methods

An **abstract class** is a class that cannot be instantiated directly. It serves as a **blueprint** for other classes. Abstract classes are meant to be inherited by other classes, which are then responsible for providing implementations for the abstract methods. The purpose of an abstract class is to provide a common interface and ensure that certain methods are implemented in the subclasses.

Key Points:

1. **Cannot be instantiated directly**: You cannot create an object of an abstract class. If you try to do so, Python will raise a `TypeError`.
2. **Provides a blueprint for subclasses**: It defines a common interface for all subclasses, ensuring they implement specific methods.
3. **May contain both abstract and non-abstract methods**: An abstract class can include methods with actual implementation (i.e., non-abstract methods), as well as methods that must be overridden by subclasses (i.e., abstract methods).

What is an Abstract Method?

An **abstract method** is a method that is declared in the abstract class but does not contain any implementation. Instead, it only defines the method's signature (i.e., its name and parameters). Subclasses that inherit the abstract class **must implement the abstract methods**, otherwise, a `TypeError` will occur when trying to instantiate the subclass.

Key Points:

1. **Declared but not implemented**: Abstract methods do not contain any code in the abstract class itself.
2. **Must be overridden in subclasses**: Subclasses are required to provide an implementation for each abstract method declared in the parent class.
3. **Used to enforce a contract**: The abstract method ensures that subclasses implement specific functionality, making the system more structured and consistent.

Syntax for Abstract Classes and Methods

To define abstract classes and abstract methods in Python, we use the `abc` (Abstract Base Class) module, which provides the necessary tools to work with abstraction.

Steps to Create an Abstract Class and Abstract Method:

1. **Import the ABC class**: From the `abc` module, you need to import the `ABC` class, which serves as the base for creating abstract classes.
2. **Inherit from ABC**: Any class that needs to be abstract must inherit from the `ABC` class.
3. **Use the `@abstractmethod` decorator**: This decorator is applied to methods that should be abstract, indicating that these methods must be implemented in subclasses.

Example of Abstract Classes and Methods

Here's an example to understand how abstract classes and methods work in Python:

```
from abc import ABC, abstractmethod

# Abstract class
class Animal(ABC):
    # Abstract method
    @abstractmethod
    def make_sound(self):
        pass

# Subclass of Animal
class Dog(Animal):
    def make_sound(self):
        return "Woof!"

# Subclass of Animal
class Cat(Animal):
    def make_sound(self):
        return "Meow!"

# Instantiate objects of subclasses
dog = Dog()
cat = Cat()

print(dog.make_sound())   # Output: Woof!
print(cat.make_sound())   # Output: Meow!
```

Explanation:

1. **Animal** is an abstract class that contains the abstract method `make_sound`. The method is declared but does not have any implementation in the `Animal` class.
2. **Dog** and **Cat** are subclasses that inherit from `Animal`. Each subclass implements the `make_sound` method, providing its own functionality (e.g., "Woof!" for Dog and "Meow!" for Cat).
3. When we try to instantiate `Dog` or `Cat` and call the `make_sound` method, the appropriate behavior (sound) is returned, as expected.

What Happens if You Don't Override an Abstract Method?

If a subclass does not implement the abstract method, Python will raise a `TypeError`. This is a safeguard to ensure that the subclass adheres to the contract defined by the abstract class.

Example of Missing Implementation:

```
from abc import ABC, abstractmethod
```

```
class Animal(ABC):
    @abstractmethod
    def make_sound(self):
        pass

# Subclass without overriding the abstract method
class Bird(Animal):
    pass  # No implementation of make_sound

# Trying to instantiate Bird will raise an error
# bird = Bird()  # This will raise TypeError: Can't instantiate
abstract class Bird with abstract method make_sound
```

In this example:

- `Bird` does not provide an implementation for `make_sound`, which results in a `TypeError` when attempting to instantiate `Bird`.
- This ensures that any class inheriting from `Animal` must implement the `make_sound` method.

Abstract Class with Non-Abstract Methods

An abstract class can also contain **non-abstract methods**—methods that have a full implementation. These methods are not required to be overridden by subclasses, but they can be overridden if needed.

Example:

```
from abc import ABC, abstractmethod

class Animal(ABC):
    @abstractmethod
    def make_sound(self):
        pass

    def sleep(self):
        return "Sleeping..."

# Subclass that overrides make_sound but uses the sleep method from the
parent class
class Dog(Animal):
    def make_sound(self):
        return "Woof!"

# Creating an object of Dog
dog = Dog()
print(dog.make_sound())   # Output: Woof!
print(dog.sleep())        # Output: Sleeping...
```

In this example:

- The `Dog` class overrides the abstract method `make_sound`, but it does not need to override the `sleep` method, as it is already implemented in the `Animal` class.
- The `sleep` method is inherited directly from `Animal` and can be used by `Dog`.

Key Benefits of Using Abstract Classes and Methods

- **Enforcing a Contract**: Abstract classes define a contract for subclasses, ensuring that they implement specific methods and behavior. This leads to more structured and consistent code.
- **Code Reusability**: Abstract classes provide common functionality that can be shared among all subclasses, reducing redundancy.
- **Flexibility**: Subclasses can provide their own specialized implementations while still following the blueprint set by the abstract class.

-

3. Using the abc Module in Python

In Python, **abstract classes** and **abstract methods** are key components used to achieve **abstraction**. They help define a **blueprint** for other classes while hiding the implementation details and forcing subclasses to implement specific functionality. Let's dive deeper into both concepts.

What is an Abstract Class?

An **abstract class** is a class that cannot be instantiated directly. It serves as a **blueprint** for other classes. Abstract classes are meant to be inherited by other classes, which are then responsible for providing implementations for the abstract methods. The purpose of an abstract class is to provide a common interface and ensure that certain methods are implemented in the subclasses.

Key Points:

1. **Cannot be instantiated directly**: You cannot create an object of an abstract class. If you try to do so, Python will raise a `TypeError`.
2. **Provides a blueprint for subclasses**: It defines a common interface for all subclasses, ensuring they implement specific methods.

3. **May contain both abstract and non-abstract methods**: An abstract class can include methods with actual implementation (i.e., non-abstract methods), as well as methods that must be overridden by subclasses (i.e., abstract methods).

What is an Abstract Method?

An **abstract method** is a method that is declared in the abstract class but does not contain any implementation. Instead, it only defines the method's signature (i.e., its name and parameters). Subclasses that inherit the abstract class **must implement the abstract methods**, otherwise, a `TypeError` will occur when trying to instantiate the subclass.

Key Points:

1. **Declared but not implemented**: Abstract methods do not contain any code in the abstract class itself.
2. **Must be overridden in subclasses**: Subclasses are required to provide an implementation for each abstract method declared in the parent class.
3. **Used to enforce a contract**: The abstract method ensures that subclasses implement specific functionality, making the system more structured and consistent.

Syntax for Abstract Classes and Methods

To define abstract classes and abstract methods in Python, we use the abc (Abstract Base Class) module, which provides the necessary tools to work with abstraction.

Steps to Create an Abstract Class and Abstract Method:

1. **Import the ABC class**: From the abc module, you need to import the ABC class, which serves as the base for creating abstract classes.
2. **Inherit from ABC**: Any class that needs to be abstract must inherit from the ABC class.
3. **Use the @abstractmethod decorator**: This decorator is applied to methods that should be abstract, indicating that these methods must be implemented in subclasses.

Example of Abstract Classes and Methods

Here's an example to understand how abstract classes and methods work in Python:

```
from abc import ABC, abstractmethod
```

```python
# Abstract class
class Animal(ABC):
    # Abstract method
    @abstractmethod
    def make_sound(self):
        pass

# Subclass of Animal
class Dog(Animal):
    def make_sound(self):
        return "Woof!"

# Subclass of Animal
class Cat(Animal):
    def make_sound(self):
        return "Meow!"

# Instantiate objects of subclasses
dog = Dog()
cat = Cat()

print(dog.make_sound())   # Output: Woof!
print(cat.make_sound())   # Output: Meow!
```

Explanation:

1. **Animal** is an abstract class that contains the abstract method `make_sound`. The method is declared but does not have any implementation in the `Animal` class.
2. **Dog** and **Cat** are subclasses that inherit from `Animal`. Each subclass implements the `make_sound` method, providing its own functionality (e.g., "Woof!" for Dog and "Meow!" for Cat).
3. When we try to instantiate `Dog` or `Cat` and call the `make_sound` method, the appropriate behavior (sound) is returned, as expected.

What Happens if You Don't Override an Abstract Method?

If a subclass does not implement the abstract method, Python will raise a `TypeError`. This is a safeguard to ensure that the subclass adheres to the contract defined by the abstract class.

Example of Missing Implementation:

```python
from abc import ABC, abstractmethod

class Animal(ABC):
    @abstractmethod
    def make_sound(self):
        pass

# Subclass without overriding the abstract method
class Bird(Animal):
```

```
    pass  # No implementation of make_sound

# Trying to instantiate Bird will raise an error
# bird = Bird()  # This will raise TypeError: Can't instantiate
abstract class Bird with abstract method make_sound
```

In this example:

- `Bird` does not provide an implementation for `make_sound`, which results in a `TypeError` when attempting to instantiate `Bird`.
- This ensures that any class inheriting from `Animal` must implement the `make_sound` method.

Abstract Class with Non-Abstract Methods

An abstract class can also contain **non-abstract methods**—methods that have a full implementation. These methods are not required to be overridden by subclasses, but they can be overridden if needed.

Example:

```
from abc import ABC, abstractmethod

class Animal(ABC):
    @abstractmethod
    def make_sound(self):
        pass

    def sleep(self):
        return "Sleeping..."

# Subclass that overrides make_sound but uses the sleep method from the
parent class
class Dog(Animal):
    def make_sound(self):
        return "Woof!"

# Creating an object of Dog
dog = Dog()
print(dog.make_sound())    # Output: Woof!
print(dog.sleep())         # Output: Sleeping...
```

In this example:

- The `Dog` class overrides the abstract method `make_sound`, but it does not need to override the `sleep` method, as it is already implemented in the `Animal` class.
- The `sleep` method is inherited directly from `Animal` and can be used by `Dog`.

Key Benefits of Using Abstract Classes and Methods

- **Enforcing a Contract**: Abstract classes define a contract for subclasses, ensuring that they implement specific methods and behavior. This leads to more structured and consistent code.
- **Code Reusability**: Abstract classes provide common functionality that can be shared among all subclasses, reducing redundancy.
- **Flexibility**: Subclasses can provide their own specialized implementations while still following the blueprint set by the abstract class.

---

4. Examples of Abstraction in Real-world Problems

Example 1: Banking System

- **Abstraction** in a **banking system** can be seen when we interact with different banking services, such as **withdrawal**, **deposit**, **checking balance**, etc., without knowing the internal workings of these transactions.
- You do not need to understand how the bank internally manages the accounts, validates transactions, or maintains security; you simply use the interface provided (e.g., ATM, online banking).

```
from abc import ABC, abstractmethod

class Account(ABC):
    @abstractmethod
    def balance(self):
        pass

    @abstractmethod
    def withdraw(self, amount):
        pass

    @abstractmethod
    def deposit(self, amount):
        pass

class SavingsAccount(Account):
    def __init__(self, balance):
        self.balance_amount = balance

    def balance(self):
        return self.balance_amount

    def withdraw(self, amount):
        if amount <= self.balance_amount:
            self.balance_amount -= amount
            return f"Withdrew {amount}"
        return "Insufficient balance"

    def deposit(self, amount):
```

```
        self.balance_amount += amount
        return f"Deposited {amount}"

# Creating an object of SavingsAccount
account = SavingsAccount(1000)
print(account.balance())     # Output: 1000
print(account.withdraw(200))    # Output: Withdrew 200
print(account.balance())     # Output: 800
```

- **Abstraction in Action**: The user only interacts with the methods like `withdraw`, `deposit`, and `balance`, without needing to know how these operations are internally handled.

Example 2: Car Interface

- **Abstraction** can be seen in a **car** interface where the user can **start**, **stop**, and **accelerate** the car without knowing how the car engine works or how these actions are executed.

```
from abc import ABC, abstractmethod

class Vehicle(ABC):
    @abstractmethod
    def start(self):
        pass

    @abstractmethod
    def stop(self):
        pass

class Car(Vehicle):
    def start(self):
        return "Car started."

    def stop(self):
        return "Car stopped."

# Creating a Car object
car = Car()
print(car.start())    # Output: Car started.
print(car.stop())     # Output: Car stopped.
```

- **Abstraction in Action**: The user only knows that the car has a `start` and `stop` functionality, but does not need to understand how these operations interact with the engine or other internal systems.

Key Benefits of Abstraction

- **Improved Focus on Essential Details**: By hiding unnecessary implementation details, abstraction allows users to focus on the essential parts of the system.
- **Code Reusability**: Abstract classes can be reused and extended by subclasses.

- **Flexibility and Maintainability**: Since implementation details are hidden, it is easier to modify the internal workings of a class without affecting the external interface.

MCQ

What is Abstraction?

1. **What does Abstraction in Object-Oriented Programming mean?**
   - ○ A) Hiding the complexity and showing only the essential details.
   - ○ B) Showing all the details and hiding none.
   - ○ C) Making a class or method private.
   - ○ D) Implementing multiple classes with different names.

   Answer: A

2. **Which of the following is a key characteristic of Abstraction?**
   - ○ A) It hides implementation details and exposes only the functionality.
   - ○ B) It is used to implement inheritance.
   - ○ C) It focuses on the implementation details.
   - ○ D) It is used for method overloading.

   Answer: A

3. **Which of the following is NOT an example of abstraction?**
   - ○ A) Hiding implementation details in a class.
   - ○ B) Using an interface in Java to hide method implementations.
   - ○ C) Creating a class that contains concrete implementations of all methods.
   - ○ D) Using an abstract class in Python.

   Answer: C

4. **What is the main purpose of Abstraction in programming?**
   - ○ A) To increase the complexity of the code.
   - ○ B) To hide the internal working details and expose only the relevant information.
   - ○ C) To decrease the flexibility of the code.
   - ○ D) To make the code slower.

   Answer: B

5. **Which of the following is an abstraction mechanism?**
   - ○ A) Abstract Classes
   - ○ B) Interfaces
   - ○ C) Both A and B
   - ○ D) None of the above

Answer: C

6. **Which of the following is an example of abstraction in real-world systems?**
   - o   A) A TV remote control that hides the internal workings of the TV.
   - o   B) The engine of a car.
   - o   C) The process of sending an email.
   - o   D) None of the above.

Answer: A

7. **What does Abstraction allow the programmer to focus on?**
   - o   A) Internal logic of the program.
   - o   B) The user interface.
   - o   C) High-level functionality and behavior without worrying about details.
   - o   D) Memory management.

Answer: C

8. **In Abstraction, which of the following is hidden?**
   - o   A) Details of how a function or class works.
   - o   B) The implementation of low-level code.
   - o   C) Both A and B.
   - o   D) None of the above.

Answer: C

Abstract Classes and Methods

9. **What is an abstract class?**
   - o   A) A class that has no methods.
   - o   B) A class that cannot be instantiated and contains abstract methods.
   - o   C) A class that is already implemented.
   - o   D) A class that can be instantiated.

Answer: B

10. **What is the purpose of an abstract method in a class?**

   - •   A) To provide a method implementation.
   - •   B) To define a method without implementation, forcing subclasses to provide one.
   - •   C) To override a method in a parent class.
   - •   D) To make the class abstract.

Answer: B

11. **Can you create an instance of an abstract class in Python?**

- A) Yes, if it contains implemented methods.
- B) Yes, if all methods are abstract.
- C) No, you cannot create an instance of an abstract class.
- D) Yes, if it has a constructor.

Answer: C

12. **What must a subclass do if it inherits from an abstract class with abstract methods?**

- A) Implement all abstract methods.
- B) Leave the abstract methods unimplemented.
- C) Provide an implementation for at least one abstract method.
- D) None of the above.

Answer: A

13. **Which of the following will result in a TypeError?**

- A) Creating an object of a subclass that implements all abstract methods.
- B) Creating an object of an abstract class.
- C) Creating an object of an abstract class with no abstract methods.
- D) None of the above.

Answer: B

14. **What will happen if an abstract method is not implemented in the subclass?**

- A) The program will run with no issues.
- B) The subclass will be able to instantiate the object.
- C) A `TypeError` will occur when attempting to instantiate the subclass.
- D) The program will ignore the abstract method.

Answer: C

15. **Which of the following is true about abstract methods?**

- A) They can have an implementation in the abstract class.
- B) They must be overridden in the subclass.
- C) They cannot have parameters.
- D) They are not necessary for abstract classes.

Answer: B

Using the abc Module in Python

16. **Which module in Python is used to define abstract classes and methods?**

- A) `abstract`
- B) `abc`
- C) `abstractclass`
- D) `abcmodule`

Answer: B

17. **Which class from the `abc` module is used to create an abstract class in Python?**

- A) `AbstractClass`
- B) `ABC`
- C) `Base`
- D) `AbstractBaseClass`

Answer: B

18. **What is the decorator used to define abstract methods in Python?**

- A) `@abstract`
- B) `@abstractmethod`
- C) `@method`
- D) `@abstract_function`

Answer: B

19. **Which of the following is a correct implementation of an abstract class in Python using the `abc` module?**

```
from abc import ABC, abstractmethod
class MyAbstractClass(ABC):
    @abstractmethod
    def my_method(self):
        pass
```

- A) The code is correct, and `MyAbstractClass` is abstract.
- B) The code is incorrect because `@abstractmethod` should not be used on a method.
- C) The code is incorrect because the abstract class is not instantiated.
- D) The code is correct, but `ABC` should be replaced with `object`.

Answer: A

20. **Which of the following can be included in an abstract class?**

- A) Only abstract methods.
- B) Both abstract methods and concrete methods (methods with implementation).
- C) Only concrete methods.
- D) Only constructors.

Answer: B

21. **In the abc module, which of the following would correctly instantiate a subclass of an abstract class?**

- A) `my_object = MyAbstractClass()`
- B) `my_object = MyConcreteClass()`
- C) `my_object = MyAbstractClass.subclass()`
- D) `my_object = MyConcreteClass.subclass()`

Answer: B

22. **What will happen if you try to instantiate an abstract class with unimplemented abstract methods?**

- A) It will work and run with a default implementation.
- B) A TypeError will occur.
- C) The program will raise a SyntaxError.
- D) It will run without any errors.

Answer: B

23. **Can abstract methods have default implementations in the abstract class in Python?**

- A) Yes, abstract methods can have default implementations.
- B) No, abstract methods cannot have implementations in the abstract class.
- C) Yes, but only if the subclass does not implement them.
- D) No, abstract methods must always be defined in subclasses.

Answer: B

24. **Which of the following is an example of how to define an abstract method in Python using the abc module?**

```
from abc import ABC, abstractmethod
class Vehicle(ABC):
    @abstractmethod
    def start(self):
        pass
```

- A) The `start` method is an abstract method, and `Vehicle` is abstract.

- B) The code is incorrect because abstract methods cannot have parameters.
- C) The code will not work because `Vehicle` is not instantiated.
- D) The `@abstractmethod` decorator is incorrectly used.

Answer: A

25. **What will happen if a subclass does not implement an abstract method?**

- A) The subclass will inherit the abstract method's implementation from the parent class.
- B) The program will automatically implement the method.
- C) A `TypeError` will occur when trying to instantiate the subclass.
- D) The subclass can still be instantiated without the method.

Answer: C

Conclusion

Abstraction is a core principle of object-oriented programming that helps to reduce complexity by exposing only the necessary functionality and hiding the internal workings. Using abstract classes and methods, along with Python's `abc` module, developers can design flexible and maintainable systems that promote modularity and code reuse. Abstraction is widely used in real-world applications, such as banking systems, vehicle interfaces, and user interfaces, where only essential operations are provided to the user.

CHAPTER 7: SPECIAL METHODS AND OPERATOR OVERLOADING

Special Methods and Operator Overloading

In Python, **special methods** (also known as **magic methods** or **dunder methods**) are methods that are surrounded by double underscores (__). These methods allow you to customize how objects of a class behave in certain situations, like printing, adding, comparing, or converting to a string. Operator overloading is the ability to define how standard operators (such as +, -, *, etc.) behave when applied to instances of custom classes.

Let's dive deeper into the key concepts of special methods and operator overloading in Python:

---

1. What are Special Methods (Magic Methods)?

Special methods in Python are predefined methods that Python calls automatically when certain operations are performed on objects. They allow you to define or modify the behavior of your class for built-in functions, operators, and other expressions. These methods are generally not invoked directly but are used implicitly by Python under specific circumstances.

Here are some of the most commonly used special methods in Python:

1.1 Constructor Methods

- **__init__**: The constructor method is called when an object is instantiated (i.e., when you create an object). It initializes the object's attributes.

```python
class Person:
    def __init__(self, name, age):
        self.name = name
        self.age = age

# Create an object
p = Person("Alice", 30)
```

1.2 String Representation Methods

- **__str__**: This method is called when you use str() or print() on an object. It defines the string representation of the object for human-readable output.

```python
class Person:
    def __str__(self):
        return f"Person(name={self.name}, age={self.age})"
```

- **`__repr__`**: This method defines how an object is represented when it's printed in the console or used in the REPL. It is typically intended for developers and should ideally be a valid Python expression that can recreate the object.

```python
Copy code
class Person:
    def __repr__(self):
        return f"Person('{self.name}', {self.age})"
```

1.3 Arithmetic Operators

Special methods allow you to customize arithmetic operations like addition, subtraction, multiplication, etc. These are known as **operator overloading**. Python calls these methods when you use operators like +, -, *, /, etc., on objects.

- **`__add__`**: Called when you use the + operator.
- **`__sub__`**: Called when you use the – operator.
- **`__mul__`**: Called when you use the * operator.
- **`__truediv__`**: Called when you use the / operator.

Example:

```python
class Point:
    def __init__(self, x, y):
        self.x = x
        self.y = y

    def __add__(self, other):
        return Point(self.x + other.x, self.y + other.y)

    def __repr__(self):
        return f"Point({self.x}, {self.y})"

# Creating two Point objects
p1 = Point(2, 3)
p2 = Point(1, 4)

# Using the overloaded + operator
p3 = p1 + p2
print(p3)   # Output: Point(3, 7)
```

1.4 Comparison Operators

Python allows you to define how comparison operators work on your objects by implementing the following special methods:

- **`__eq__`**: Defines behavior for the equality operator (==).
- **`__ne__`**: Defines behavior for the not-equal operator (!=).
- **`__lt__`**: Defines behavior for the less-than operator (<).
- **`__le__`**: Defines behavior for the less-than or equal operator (<=).

- **__gt__**: Defines behavior for the greater-than operator (>).
- **__ge__**: Defines behavior for the greater-than or equal operator (>=).

Example:

```
class Person:
    def __init__(self, name, age):
        self.name = name
        self.age = age

    def __eq__(self, other):
        return self.age == other.age

# Create two Person objects
p1 = Person("Alice", 30)
p2 = Person("Bob", 30)

print(p1 == p2)   # Output: True
```

1.5 Container Methods

Python provides special methods to allow custom objects to behave like containers (such as lists, dictionaries, or sets). For example:

- **__len__**: Allows you to define the behavior of the len() function.
- **__getitem__**: Allows indexing into the object using square brackets ([]).
- **__setitem__**: Allows assignment to an index using square brackets ([]).
- **__delitem__**: Allows deletion of an index using the del keyword.

Example:

```
class MyList:
    def __init__(self, items):
        self.items = items

    def __len__(self):
        return len(self.items)

    def __getitem__(self, index):
        return self.items[index]

# Create an object of MyList
mylist = MyList([1, 2, 3, 4])

print(len(mylist))   # Output: 4
print(mylist[2])     # Output: 3
```

2. Operator Overloading in Python

Operator overloading allows you to define how standard operators like +, -, *, etc., should behave when applied to objects of a class. By implementing special methods in your class, you can control the behavior of these operators for your custom objects.

Common Operator Overloading Methods:

1. **__add__**: Defines behavior for + operator.
2. **__sub__**: Defines behavior for – operator.
3. **__mul__**: Defines behavior for * operator.
4. **__truediv__**: Defines behavior for / operator.
5. **__floordiv__**: Defines behavior for // operator.
6. **__mod__**: Defines behavior for % operator.
7. **__pow__**: Defines behavior for ** operator (power).

Example: Overloading the + operator

```python
class Vector:
    def __init__(self, x, y):
        self.x = x
        self.y = y

    def __add__(self, other):
        return Vector(self.x + other.x, self.y + other.y)

    def __repr__(self):
        return f"Vector({self.x}, {self.y})"

# Create two Vector objects
v1 = Vector(1, 2)
v2 = Vector(3, 4)

# Using the overloaded + operator
v3 = v1 + v2
print(v3)  # Output: Vector(4, 6)
```

Here, we overloaded the + operator to add two vectors together. When v1 + v2 is evaluated, Python calls the __add__ method.

Example: Overloading the * operator for Matrix Multiplication

```python
class Matrix:
    def __init__(self, data):
        self.data = data

    def __mul__(self, other):
        result = []
        for i in range(len(self.data)):
            row = []
            for j in range(len(other.data[0])):
```

```python
            value = sum(self.data[i][k] * other.data[k][j] for k in
range(len(other.data)))
                row.append(value)
            result.append(row)
        return Matrix(result)

    def __repr__(self):
        return f"Matrix({self.data})"

# Create two matrices
m1 = Matrix([[1, 2], [3, 4]])
m2 = Matrix([[5, 6], [7, 8]])

# Matrix multiplication using the overloaded * operator
m3 = m1 * m2
print(m3)   # Output: Matrix([[19, 22], [43, 50]])
```

In this example, we overloaded the * operator for matrix multiplication. The result is the product of two matrices.

---

3. Real-World Applications of Special Methods and Operator Overloading

Special methods and operator overloading are useful for building intuitive, user-friendly APIs and for customizing how your objects interact with built-in Python functions.

Real-World Examples:

1. **Custom Data Structures**: You can implement data structures like lists, sets, or maps by overloading methods like __getitem__, __setitem__, __delitem__, and __len__.
2. **Complex Number Arithmetic**: In scientific computing or graphics, you can overload arithmetic operators to work with complex numbers or vectors in an intuitive way.
3. **Matrix Operations**: As shown in the example above, operator overloading allows you to implement matrix multiplication, addition, and other operations.
4. **Custom Containers**: By overloading container methods, you can create custom collection classes that behave like built-in Python collections (e.g., list, dictionary).
5. **GUI Frameworks**: In GUI frameworks, special methods like __str__, __repr__, and others can be used to customize how widgets are represented and interacted with.

1. Understanding Python's Special Methods (`__str__`, `__repr__`, etc.)

Python provides several special methods to modify or enhance the behavior of objects in certain situations. These methods are often called **dunder** (double underscore) methods because their names begin and end with double underscores (__).

Common Special Methods

- **`__str__`**: This method defines how an object is represented as a string. It is called when you use the `str()` function or print an object.
  - Example: Printing a string representation of an object.
- **`__repr__`**: This method defines how an object should be represented as a string when viewed in the interpreter or when using the `repr()` function. The goal of `__repr__` is to return a string that, if passed to `eval()`, would ideally create an object that is equal to the original.
  - Example: Returning a formal, unambiguous string representation of an object.
- **`__init__`**: This is the constructor method, called when a new instance of a class is created. It initializes the object's attributes.
- **`__add__`, `__sub__`, `__mul__`, etc.**: These are methods for overloading arithmetic operators. For example, `__add__` defines how the + operator works for objects of the class.
- **`__eq__`**: This method is called when you use the equality operator (==) to compare two objects.
- **`__len__`**: This method is called when the `len()` function is used on an object. It should return an integer.
- **`__getitem__`**: This method is called when an object is accessed like a list or dictionary, i.e., `obj[key]`.
- **`__del__`**: This method is called when an object is about to be destroyed or deleted.

Example: `__str__` vs. `__repr__`

```python
class Person:
    def __init__(self, name, age):
        self.name = name
        self.age = age

    def __str__(self):
        return f"Person's name is {self.name} and age is {self.age}"

    def __repr__(self):
        return f"Person('{self.name}', {self.age})"

# Create an object
p = Person("John", 30)

# Using str() or print()
print(str(p))   # Output: Person's name is John and age is 30
```

```
# Using repr()
print(repr(p))   # Output: Person('John', 30)
```

- __str__ is intended for human-readable string output (i.e., when you print an object).
- __repr__ is intended for debugging and machine-readable output.

2. Implementing Operator Overloading

Operator overloading in Python allows you to define how operators (such as +, -, *, etc.) work when applied to objects of custom classes. This makes your classes more intuitive to use, as it allows objects of your class to interact with operators just like built-in types (e.g., integers, strings, etc.).

By implementing **special methods** (also known as magic or dunder methods) in your class, you can customize the behavior of operators. These methods are invoked automatically when operators are used on objects of the class.

Common Operator Overloading Methods

Each operator in Python has a corresponding special method that you can define in your custom class. Here are some of the most commonly used special methods for operator overloading:

1. __add__: Overloads the + operator.
   o This method defines the behavior of the + operator when applied to objects of the class.
2. __sub__: Overloads the – operator.
   o This method defines the behavior of the – operator for objects of the class.
3. __mul__: Overloads the * operator.
   o This method defines the behavior of the * operator for objects of the class.
4. __truediv__: Overloads the / operator.
   o This method defines the behavior of the division operator / for objects of the class.
5. __eq__: Overloads the == operator.
   o This method defines the behavior of the equality operator == when comparing objects.
6. __lt__: Overloads the < operator.
   o This method defines the behavior of the less-than operator < for comparisons between objects.
7. __gt__: Overloads the > operator.
   o This method defines the behavior of the greater-than operator > for comparisons between objects.

Example of Overloading the + Operator

In this example, we'll define a `Point` class where the + operator will add two `Point` objects. We'll achieve this by overloading the `__add__` method, which will add the corresponding `x` and `y` coordinates of two `Point` objects.

Code Example: Overloading the + Operator

```python
class Point:
    def __init__(self, x, y):
        self.x = x
        self.y = y

    def __add__(self, other):
        # Adding corresponding x and y coordinates
        return Point(self.x + other.x, self.y + other.y)

    def __repr__(self):
        return f"Point({self.x}, {self.y})"

# Create two Point objects
p1 = Point(1, 2)
p2 = Point(3, 4)

# Adding two Point objects using the overloaded + operator
p3 = p1 + p2

# Output the result
print(p3)   # Output: Point(4, 6)
```

Explanation:

- The `__add__` method is defined in the `Point` class. When we use the + operator between two `Point` objects, Python calls this method.
- The `__add__` method takes another `Point` object (`other`) as an argument and returns a new `Point` object where the `x` and `y` coordinates are the sum of the corresponding coordinates of `p1` and `p2`.
- When we print the result, the `__repr__` method is called, which gives us a readable string representation of the `Point` object.

In this case, `p1 + p2` results in a new `Point` object with coordinates `(4, 6)`.

Other Operator Overloading Examples

Let's explore some other common operators that can be overloaded by defining corresponding special methods in the class.

1. Overloading the – (Subtraction) Operator

The `__sub__` method allows you to define the behavior of the subtraction operator (-) for your custom objects.

```
class Point:
    def __init__(self, x, y):
        self.x = x
        self.y = y

    def __sub__(self, other):
        # Subtracting corresponding x and y coordinates
        return Point(self.x - other.x, self.y - other.y)

    def __repr__(self):
        return f"Point({self.x}, {self.y})"

# Create two Point objects
p1 = Point(5, 7)
p2 = Point(3, 4)

# Subtracting two Point objects using the overloaded - operator
p3 = p1 - p2

print(p3)   # Output: Point(2, 3)
```

Explanation:

- The `__sub__` method defines the subtraction behavior for `Point` objects. It subtracts the `x` and `y` coordinates of one `Point` object from another and returns a new `Point` object.

2. Overloading the * (Multiplication) Operator

The `__mul__` method allows you to define how the * operator behaves for custom objects.

```
class Point:
    def __init__(self, x, y):
        self.x = x
        self.y = y

    def __mul__(self, scalar):
        # Multiplying the point's coordinates by a scalar value
        return Point(self.x * scalar, self.y * scalar)

    def __repr__(self):
        return f"Point({self.x}, {self.y})"

# Create a Point object
p1 = Point(2, 3)

# Multiplying a Point object by a scalar
p2 = p1 * 3
```

```
print(p2)   # Output: Point(6, 9)
```

Explanation:

- The __mul__ method is used to multiply the Point object by a scalar. Here, the x and y coordinates of the Point are multiplied by a scalar value (in this case, 3).

3. Overloading the / (Division) Operator

The __truediv__ method defines how the division operator / behaves for custom objects.

```
class Point:
    def __init__(self, x, y):
        self.x = x
        self.y = y

    def __truediv__(self, scalar):
        # Dividing the point's coordinates by a scalar value
        return Point(self.x / scalar, self.y / scalar)

    def __repr__(self):
        return f"Point({self.x}, {self.y})"

# Create a Point object
p1 = Point(6, 9)

# Dividing a Point object by a scalar
p2 = p1 / 3

print(p2)   # Output: Point(2.0, 3.0)
```

Explanation:

- The __truediv__ method allows division of a Point object by a scalar, resulting in a new Point object with the x and y coordinates divided by the scalar.

Real-World Example: Complex Numbers

Let's now look at an example involving complex numbers, where we overload the + operator to add the real and imaginary parts of two complex numbers.

Code Example: Overloading the + Operator for Complex Numbers

```
class ComplexNumber:
    def __init__(self, real, imag):
        self.real = real
        self.imag = imag
```

```python
    def __add__(self, other):
        # Adding the real and imaginary parts of two complex numbers
        return ComplexNumber(self.real + other.real, self.imag +
other.imag)

    def __repr__(self):
        return f"{self.real} + {self.imag}i"

# Create two complex numbers
c1 = ComplexNumber(2, 3)
c2 = ComplexNumber(1, 4)

# Adding two complex numbers
c3 = c1 + c2

print(c3)   # Output: 3 + 7i
```

Explanation:

- In this example, we overloaded the + operator for the ComplexNumber class. The __add__ method adds the real and imaginary parts of two complex numbers, creating a new ComplexNumber object with the sum.

---

3. Real-world Applications of Special Methods

Special methods play an essential role in customizing the behavior of objects in Python, and they are used in real-world applications for a variety of purposes:

1. Customizing Object String Representations

In a real-world application, when you work with complex data structures or objects, overriding __str__ and __repr__ allows you to control how objects are printed or represented in logs, making debugging and logging much more user-friendly.

- **Example**: In a banking application, we can use __str__ to format a customer's account details for display:

```python
class BankAccount:
    def __init__(self, account_number, balance):
        self.account_number = account_number
        self.balance = balance

    def __str__(self):
        return f"BankAccount({self.account_number}): Balance:
${self.balance}"

# Create a BankAccount object
account = BankAccount("12345", 1000)
```

```
print(account)   # Output: BankAccount(12345): Balance: $1000
```

2. Custom Collections and Containers

When you create custom collections or containers (like lists, sets, dictionaries), overloading methods like __len__, __getitem__, and __iter__ allows you to define how the collection behaves in loops and with built-in functions.

```
class MyList:
    def __init__(self, data):
        self.data = data

    def __len__(self):
        return len(self.data)

    def __getitem__(self, index):
        return self.data[index]

# Create a MyList object
mylist = MyList([1, 2, 3])

print(len(mylist))   # Output: 3
print(mylist[1])     # Output: 2
```

Here, the __len__ method allows you to use len() on your custom collection, and the __getitem__ method allows indexing into the collection.

3. Customizing Arithmetic Operations

In applications that require mathematical or financial calculations (such as complex numbers or 2D vectors), operator overloading is commonly used to define how objects behave with arithmetic operators.

For example, in a **2D vector class**, overloading the +, -, and other arithmetic operators allows you to write cleaner and more readable code when performing vector math.

MCQ

1. Understanding Python's Special Methods (str, repr, etc.)

1. **What is the purpose of the __str__ method in Python?** a) To represent the object as a string for debugging purposes
   b) To define the object's string representation for print() and str()
   c) To return a string with the object's memory address
   d) To compare two objects
   Answer: b) To define the object's string representation for print() and str()

2. **Which method is used to define the official string representation of an object for debugging?** a) `__str__`
   b) `__repr__`
   c) `__add__`
   d) `__call__`
   Answer: b) `__repr__`

3. **What is the output of the following code?**

```python
Copy code
class Person:
    def __init__(self, name):
        self.name = name

    def __str__(self):
        return f"Person: {self.name}"

p = Person("Alice")
print(p)
```

   a) `Person`
   b) `Alice`
   c) `Person: Alice`
   d) `Alice: Person`
   Answer: c) `Person: Alice`

4. **Which special method is automatically called when you use the `print()` function on an object?** a) `__call__`
   b) `__str__`
   c) `__repr__`
   d) `__len__`
   Answer: b) `__str__`

5. **What is the primary difference between `__str__` and `__repr__` methods?** a) `__str__` is for object creation, while `__repr__` is for object comparison
   b) `__str__` is used for informal display, while `__repr__` is for debugging and development
   c) `__str__` is used to check object equality, while `__repr__` is used for sorting
   d) `__str__` is used to define object comparison, while `__repr__` is for method overloading

Answer: b) __str__ is used for informal display, while __repr__ is for debugging and development

6. **What will the following code output?**

```
class Circle:
    def __init__(self, radius):
        self.radius = radius

    def __repr__(self):
        return f"Circle(radius={self.radius})"

c = Circle(5)
print(c)
```

a) `Circle(5)`
b) `Circle(radius=5)`
c) `5`
d) `Circle`
Answer: b) `Circle(radius=5)`

7. **Which special method is used to get the length of an object in Python?** a) `__init__`
b) `__len__`
c) `__str__`
d) `__call__`
Answer: b) `__len__`

8. **What is the purpose of the __del__ method in Python?** a) To define how objects are compared
b) To initialize objects
c) To define the destructor for an object
d) To define the addition operator
Answer: c) To define the destructor for an object

9. **Which of the following is true about the __call__ special method?** a) It is used to define object comparison
b) It makes an object callable like a function
c) It defines the object's string representation
d) It is used to define arithmetic operations
Answer: b) It makes an object callable like a function

10. **Which special method is invoked when an object is used in a `for` loop?** a) `__iter__`
    b) `__getitem__`
    c) `__next__`
    d) `__call__`
    Answer: a) `__iter__`

2. Implementing Operator Overloading

11. **What does the `__add__` method do in operator overloading?** a) Defines the behavior for the addition operator (+)
    b) Defines the behavior for the multiplication operator (*)
    c) Defines the behavior for the equality operator (==)
    d) Defines the behavior for the subtraction operator (-)
    Answer: a) Defines the behavior for the addition operator (+)

12. **Which of the following special methods is used to overload the == operator?**
    a) `__lt__`
    b) `__eq__`
    c) `__add__`
    d) `__ne__`
    Answer: b) `__eq__`

13. **Which operator can be overloaded using the `__mul__` method?** a) + (Addition)
    b) - (Subtraction)
    c) * (Multiplication)
    d) / (Division)
    Answer: c) * (Multiplication)

14. **How do you define the behavior for the <= operator in Python?** a) By using the `__lt__` method
    b) By using the `__le__` method
    c) By using the `__eq__` method
    d) By using the `__ge__` method
    Answer: b) By using the `__le__` method

15. **Which method is called when the + operator is used between two objects in Python?** a) __call__

    b) __add__

    c) __sub__

    d) __mul__

    Answer: b) __add__

16. **What is the result of the following code?**

```python
class Point:
    def __init__(self, x, y):
        self.x = x
        self.y = y

    def __add__(self, other):
        return Point(self.x + other.x, self.y + other.y)

p1 = Point(2, 3)
p2 = Point(4, 5)
p3 = p1 + p2
print(p3.x, p3.y)
```

    a) 6 8

    b) 2 3

    c) 4 5

    d) 6 5

    Answer: a) 6 8

17. **Which operator is overloaded using the __sub__ method?** a) +

    b) –

    c) *

    d) /

    Answer: b) –

18. **What does the __truediv__ method overload?** a) * (Multiplication)

    b) / (Division)

    c) + (Addition)

    d) == (Equality)

    Answer: b) / (Division)

19. **Which of the following is the correct method to overload the > operator?** a) `__lt__`
    b) `__gt__`
    c) `__le__`
    d) `__eq__`
    Answer: b) `__gt__`

20. **In operator overloading, which method is invoked when you use the * operator?** a) `__mul__`
    b) `__add__`
    c) `__sub__`
    d) `__truediv__`
    Answer: a) `__mul__`

3. Real-world Applications of Special Methods

21. **Which of the following is a common real-world use of operator overloading in Python?** a) Overloading arithmetic operators to perform matrix operations
    b) Overloading the == operator for dictionary comparisons
    c) Overloading the + operator for string concatenation
    d) Overloading the `print()` function for object display
    Answer: a) Overloading arithmetic operators to perform matrix operations

22. **How can special methods be useful in implementing custom data types?** a) They help define the behavior of operators with custom data types
    b) They enable custom data types to support standard operations like addition, comparison, etc.
    c) They make it possible to use built-in functions with custom objects
    d) All of the above
    Answer: d) All of the above

23. **Which of the following is a real-world application of the `__call__` method in Python?** a) Making an object callable as a function
    b) Representing the object as a string
    c) Sorting objects in a list

d) Counting the number of iterations in a loop
Answer: a) Making an object callable as a function

24. **How can operator overloading be applied to custom `Fraction` objects?** a) Overload arithmetic operators like +, -, *, and / to perform fraction operations
b) Overload the equality operator == for fraction comparisons
c) Overload the string representation methods for fraction formatting
d) All of the above
Answer: d) All of the above

25. **What is the real-world application of overloading the `__repr__` method in custom classes?** a) To make debugging easier by displaying more informative object representations
b) To print a custom string representation of an object
c) To provide a readable output for data serialization
d) To compare objects efficiently
Answer: a) To make debugging easier by displaying more informative object representations

Conclusion

Special methods and operator overloading in Python allow for a high level of customization in how objects behave. Whether you're building complex data structures, handling arithmetic operations, or customizing the string representations of objects, these features provide an intuitive way to make your code more readable, maintainable, and efficient.

CHAPTER 8: WORKING WITH COLLECTIONS IN OOP

Object-Oriented Programming (OOP) allows you to structure code into logical components called "objects." Collections like lists, tuples, and dictionaries are fundamental to handling multiple pieces of data. In OOP, managing and interacting with these collections within classes allows us to represent complex data structures and offers various ways to manipulate and access the data. In this chapter, we will explore how to manage lists, tuples, and dictionaries within classes, as well as how to iterate through objects using special methods such as __iter__ and __next__. Finally, we'll look at some practical examples to bring these concepts together.

1. Managing Lists, Tuples, and Dictionaries within Classes

In Python, collections like lists, tuples, and dictionaries are commonly used to store multiple values. When working within classes, these collections can be used as attributes (also known as instance variables) to store and manage data. Let's explore each collection type (lists, tuples, and dictionaries) in the context of object-oriented programming (OOP) and see how they can be effectively utilized within classes.

Managing Lists within Classes

A **list** is a mutable, ordered collection of items in Python. Lists allow duplicate elements, and their size can change dynamically, making them ideal for storing an ordered sequence of items. Lists are perfect for use cases where:

- The order of items matters.
- Items may need to be added, modified, or removed.

Using Lists in Classes

You can use lists to store a group of related items as part of an object. For example, in the Student class, you may need to store a list of subjects.

Example:

```python
class Student:
    def __init__(self, name):
        self.name = name
        self.subjects = []  # List to store subjects

    def add_subject(self, subject):
        self.subjects.append(subject)
```

```
    def get_subjects(self):
        return self.subjects

# Create an instance of Student
student = Student("John")
student.add_subject("Math")
student.add_subject("Science")

print(student.get_subjects())   # Output: ['Math', 'Science']
```

Explanation:

- The `subjects` attribute is a list that stores subjects for each student.
- The `add_subject` method appends a new subject to the `subjects` list.
- The `get_subjects` method returns the list of subjects stored in the `subjects` attribute.

Benefits of using a list:

- You can easily modify the list, such as adding, removing, or changing elements.
- The order of subjects is preserved, and the list can dynamically grow or shrink as subjects are added or removed.

Managing Tuples within Classes

A **tuple** is similar to a list, but it is **immutable**, meaning its contents cannot be changed once it is created. Tuples are ideal when you want to store a fixed collection of items that should not be modified, such as coordinates, days of the week, or constants.

Using Tuples in Classes

Tuples can be used in classes to store fixed pairs of values or constants that shouldn't change during the life of an object. For example, in a `Point` class, you can use a tuple to store the x and y coordinates.

Example:

```
class Point:
    def __init__(self, x, y):
        self.coordinates = (x, y)   # Tuple to store coordinates

    def get_coordinates(self):
        return self.coordinates

# Create an instance of Point
point = Point(5, 7)
print(point.get_coordinates())   # Output: (5, 7)
```

Explanation:

- The `coordinates` attribute is a tuple that stores two values, x and y, representing the point's coordinates.
- The `get_coordinates` method returns the tuple containing the coordinates.

Benefits of using a tuple:

- Since tuples are immutable, they provide a guarantee that the values they store cannot be altered after initialization. This is useful for storing data that must remain constant.
- Tuples use less memory than lists because they are immutable, making them more efficient for small fixed collections.

Managing Dictionaries within Classes

A **dictionary** is an unordered collection of key-value pairs. In Python, dictionaries are widely used for scenarios where you need to associate unique keys with values. This allows for efficient lookups, additions, and modifications based on keys.

Using Dictionaries in Classes

Dictionaries can be used within a class to store data where each item is associated with a unique identifier (key). For example, in an `Employee` class, you might store salary details by month using a dictionary where the month names are the keys, and the salaries are the values.

Example:

```
class Employee:
    def __init__(self, name):
        self.name = name
        self.salary_details = {}  # Dictionary to store salary records

    def add_salary(self, month, salary):
        self.salary_details[month] = salary

    def get_salary(self, month):
        return self.salary_details.get(month, "No record")

# Create an instance of Employee
employee = Employee("Alice")
employee.add_salary("January", 5000)
employee.add_salary("February", 5500)
```

```
print(employee.get_salary("January"))   # Output: 5000
print(employee.get_salary("March"))     # Output: No record
```

Explanation:

- The `salary_details` attribute is a dictionary where the **month** is the key and the **salary** is the value.
- The `add_salary` method adds a salary for a specific month.
- The `get_salary` method retrieves the salary for a given month using the `get` method of the dictionary, which allows specifying a default value (in this case, `"No record"` if the month is not found).

Benefits of using a dictionary:

- Dictionaries provide fast lookups by key. When you need to associate unique keys with corresponding values, dictionaries are an efficient and scalable choice.
- You can easily add, update, or remove entries from a dictionary.

Summary of Managing Lists, Tuples, and Dictionaries

- **Lists** are useful when you need an ordered, mutable collection where the order of elements is important, and changes to the data may be necessary.
- **Tuples** are ideal when the data should remain constant throughout the life of the object, making them useful for storing fixed collections of values.
- **Dictionaries** are best suited for scenarios where you need to associate unique keys with corresponding values and perform fast lookups or modifications based on those keys.

Each of these collection types serves different purposes, and their use within a class depends on the nature of the data and the requirements of the program.

2. Iterating Through Objects (`__iter__` and `__next__`)

In Python, the concept of iterators is central to iterating over a collection of elements, such as lists, tuples, or even custom objects. This is commonly done using the `for` loop, which simplifies the process of going through all the elements in an iterable object. By implementing two special methods, `__iter__` and `__next__`, you can make your custom objects iterable.

The `__iter__` Method

The __iter__ method is part of the **Iterator protocol** in Python. It is required when you want an object to be iterable. This method tells Python how to start the iteration process and returns an iterator object. Typically, the iterator object is the object itself (as in the case of the `Reverse` class example below), but it can also return another object that implements the __next__ method.

- **Return Value:** The __iter__ method should return the iterator object, which is often the object itself.
- **Purpose:** It initializes the iteration process.

The __next__ Method

The __next__ method is used to retrieve the next element in the iteration. It is called automatically by the `for` loop (or any other iteration construct). Each time the __next__ method is invoked:

- It returns the next item in the sequence.
- When there are no more items to return, it raises a `StopIteration` exception to signal the end of the iteration.
- **Return Value:** The next item in the sequence (if any).
- **Purpose:** It provides the logic for returning the next item. When there are no items left, it raises `StopIteration` to end the loop.

Example of a Custom Iterator

Here's an example that demonstrates how to use __iter__ and __next__ to create a custom iterator. In this example, we define a `Reverse` class that allows us to iterate over a string in reverse order.

```python
class Reverse:
    def __init__(self, data):
        self.data = data
        self.index = len(data)  # Start at the end of the data

    def __iter__(self):
        return self  # The iterator is the object itself

    def __next__(self):
        if self.index == 0:
            raise StopIteration  # No more elements to iterate
        self.index -= 1
        return self.data[self.index]

# Create a Reverse object
rev = Reverse('giraffe')

# Iterating through the Reverse object
for char in rev:
    print(char, end=' ')
```

Explanation:

- **__init__ Method:** Initializes the object with a string (data) and sets the index to the length of the string. The index will be used to track our position while iterating backward.
- **__iter__ Method:** Returns the object itself (self) as the iterator. This is necessary because the iterator object is typically the object itself, which will also contain the logic for getting the next item.
- **__next__ Method:** In each call, it checks if the index is 0. If it is, that means we've reached the beginning of the string and there are no more elements to return, so we raise StopIteration. Otherwise, it decrements the index and returns the character at the current position.

Output:

```
e f a r i g
```

In this output, the string "giraffe" is printed in reverse order, one character at a time, because the Reverse class is designed to iterate backwards through the string.

How Iteration Works in Python

1. **Start of the Loop:**
   - The for loop calls __iter__() on the object (in this case, the Reverse object).
   - The __iter__ method returns the object itself, which is the iterator.
2. **First Iteration:**
   - The for loop calls __next__().
   - The __next__ method returns the last character of the string, which is 'e', and decreases the index.
3. **Subsequent Iterations:**
   - The loop continues calling __next__(), which returns the next character (moving backwards in the string) until the index reaches 0.
4. **End of Iteration:**
   - Once __next__ is called and the index is 0, it raises the StopIteration exception, signaling the end of the iteration. This is handled by the for loop, and the loop terminates.

Real-World Applications of Iterators

Iterators are useful in scenarios where you need to traverse a collection or data structure in a controlled manner. Here are a few real-world examples where iterators might be applied:

- **File Reading:** You could implement a custom iterator to read a file line by line.
- **Database Queries:** Iterators can be used to fetch rows from a database in a memory-efficient way.
- **Generating Sequences:** When generating large or infinite sequences, an iterator provides a way to produce each value on demand (e.g., generating Fibonacci numbers or prime numbers).

Summary

- `__iter__`: Used to initialize the iteration. It must return an iterator object (often the object itself).
- `__next__`: Returns the next item in the sequence. When no more items are left, it raises StopIteration to signal the end of the iteration.
- **Custom Iterators:** By implementing __iter__ and __next__, you can create custom iterators for your own data structures, enabling them to be used in for loops and other iteration contexts.

This functionality allows you to create objects that behave like built-in iterables such as lists, tuples, and dictionaries, but with your own iteration logic.

---

3. Practical Examples

Let's apply the concepts of managing collections and iteration in more realistic scenarios.

Example 1: Managing a Library of Books Using Lists

In this example, we will create a class Library that holds a list of books and implements an iterator to go through the books one by one.

```python
class Book:
    def __init__(self, title, author):
        self.title = title
        self.author = author

    def __repr__(self):
        return f"Book({self.title}, {self.author})"

class Library:
```

```
    def __init__(self):
        self.books = []  # List to store books

    def add_book(self, book):
        self.books.append(book)

    def __iter__(self):
        self.index = 0  # Start iteration from the first book
        return self

    def __next__(self):
        if self.index >= len(self.books):
            raise StopIteration  # End of books list
        book = self.books[self.index]
        self.index += 1
        return book

# Create a Library object and add books
library = Library()
library.add_book(Book("1984", "George Orwell"))
library.add_book(Book("To Kill a Mockingbird", "Harper Lee"))
library.add_book(Book("The Great Gatsby", "F. Scott Fitzgerald"))

# Iterating through the books
for book in library:
    print(book)
```

Output:

```
Book(1984, George Orwell)
Book(To Kill a Mockingbird, Harper Lee)
Book(The Great Gatsby, F. Scott Fitzgerald)
```

In this example:

- The `Library` class holds a list of `Book` objects.
- The `__iter__` and `__next__` methods allow iteration over the list of books, enabling use of a `for` loop to access each book.

Example 2: Dictionary to Store Student Grades

We will create a class `Student` that uses a dictionary to store subject-wise grades and allows iteration over the subjects.

```
class Student:
    def __init__(self, name):
        self.name = name
        self.grades = {}  # Dictionary to store subject-wise grades

    def add_grade(self, subject, grade):
        self.grades[subject] = grade

    def __iter__(self):
```

```
        self.subjects = iter(self.grades.items())  # Create an iterator
for grades
        return self

    def __next__(self):
        return next(self.subjects)

# Create a Student object and add grades
student = Student("Alice")
student.add_grade("Math", 90)
student.add_grade("Science", 85)
student.add_grade("English", 88)

# Iterating through the student's grades
for subject, grade in student:
    print(f"{subject}: {grade}")
```

Output:

```
Math: 90
Science: 85
English: 88
```

In this example:

- The `Student` class uses a dictionary to store grades.
- The `__iter__` and `__next__` methods allow iteration over the dictionary items (subject, grade), providing an easy way to display the student's grades.

Example 3: Managing Lists Within a Class (Todo List)

In this example, we'll use a list to manage a to-do list, allowing us to add tasks and list all tasks.

```
class TodoList:
    def __init__(self):
        self.tasks = []  # List to store tasks

    def add_task(self, task):
        self.tasks.append(task)

    def list_tasks(self):
        return self.tasks

# Create a TodoList instance
todo = TodoList()
todo.add_task("Buy groceries")
todo.add_task("Complete homework")

print(todo.list_tasks())  # Output: ['Buy groceries', 'Complete
homework']
```

Explanation:

- `tasks` is a list that stores tasks.
- The method `add_task` adds tasks to the list, while `list_tasks` returns all tasks.

Example 4: Managing Tuples Within a Class (Circle Coordinates)

In this example, we'll store the coordinates of a circle's center as a tuple.

```
class Circle:
    def __init__(self, x, y, radius):
        self.center = (x, y)  # Tuple storing center coordinates
        self.radius = radius

    def get_center(self):
        return self.center

# Create a Circle instance
circle = Circle(5, 7, 10)
print(circle.get_center())  # Output: (5, 7)
```

Explanation:

- The `center` attribute stores the circle's center as a tuple `(x, y)`.

Example 5: Managing Dictionaries Within a Class (Student Grades)

In this example, a dictionary stores the grades of students for different subjects.

```
class StudentGrades:
    def __init__(self, name):
        self.name = name
        self.grades = {}  # Dictionary to store grades

    def add_grade(self, subject, grade):
        self.grades[subject] = grade

    def get_grade(self, subject):
        return self.grades.get(subject, "No grade available")

# Create a StudentGrades instance
student = StudentGrades("Tom")
student.add_grade("Math", 90)
student.add_grade("Science", 85)

print(student.get_grade("Math"))  # Output: 90
print(student.get_grade("History"))  # Output: No grade available
```

Explanation:

- `grades` is a dictionary where the key is the subject and the value is the grade.

Example 6: Iterating Through a Range of Numbers (Custom Range Iterator)

This example shows how to iterate over a custom range of numbers using an iterator.

```
class MyRange:
    def __init__(self, start, end):
        self.start = start
        self.end = end
        self.current = start

    def __iter__(self):
        return self

    def __next__(self):
        if self.current >= self.end:
            raise StopIteration
        self.current += 1
        return self.current - 1

# Create a MyRange instance
my_range = MyRange(1, 5)

for num in my_range:
    print(num, end=" ")   # Output: 1 2 3 4
```

Explanation:

- The `MyRange` class mimics the behavior of the built-in `range` function. It starts from `start` and goes until `end` (exclusive).
- The `__next__` method increments the `current` value until it reaches the `end`, raising `StopIteration` when done.

Example7: Iterating Through a Dictionary (Key-Value Pairs)

In this example, we iterate through a dictionary of students' names and their corresponding scores.

```
class StudentScores:
    def __init__(self):
        self.scores = {
            "Alice": 95,
```

```
            "Bob": 85,
            "Charlie": 75
        }

    def __iter__(self):
        return iter(self.scores.items())

# Create a StudentScores instance
scores = StudentScores()

for student, score in scores:
    print(f"{student}: {score}")
```

Explanation:

- The `scores` dictionary is iterated through using `__iter__`, which returns the dictionary's items as key-value pairs.

Example 8: Iterating Through a List of Tuples (Coordinate Pairs)

This example demonstrates iteration through a list of tuples containing coordinate pairs.

```
class Coordinates:
    def __init__(self):
        self.coordinates = [(1, 2), (3, 4), (5, 6)]   # List of tuples

    def __iter__(self):
        return iter(self.coordinates)

# Create a Coordinates instance
coords = Coordinates()

for x, y in coords:
    print(f"({x}, {y})", end=" ")   # Output: (1, 2) (3, 4) (5, 6)
```

Explanation:

- The `coordinates` list contains tuples, each representing a pair of coordinates. The `for` loop iterates through these pairs.

Example 9: Managing a Tuple of Employee Details

In this example, we use a tuple to store immutable employee details.

```
class Employee:
    def __init__(self, name, id, position):
```

```
        self.details = (name, id, position)    # Tuple to store employee
details

    def get_details(self):
        return self.details

# Create an Employee instance
employee = Employee("John", 101, "Manager")
print(employee.get_details())   # Output: ('John', 101, 'Manager')
```

Explanation:

- The `details` tuple stores immutable information such as `name`, `id`, and `position`.

Example 10: Iterating Through a List of Dictionaries (Student Profiles)

This example shows how to iterate through a list of dictionaries representing student profiles.

```
class StudentProfiles:
    def __init__(self):
        self.profiles = [
            {"name": "Alice", "age": 21},
            {"name": "Bob", "age": 22},
            {"name": "Charlie", "age": 23}
        ]

    def __iter__(self):
        return iter(self.profiles)

# Create a StudentProfiles instance
profiles = StudentProfiles()

for profile in profiles:
    print(profile)
```

Explanation:

- The `profiles` list contains dictionaries, each representing a student's profile. The `for` loop iterates through each dictionary, printing the details.

MCQ

Managing Lists, Tuples, and Dictionaries within Classes

1. **Which of the following is a mutable collection in Python?**
   - o a) Tuple
   - o b) Dictionary
   - o c) String
   - o d) None of the above
   - o **Answer:** b) Dictionary

2. **In a class, which of the following collections is ideal for storing an ordered collection of elements where items might need modification?**
   - o a) Tuple
   - o b) List
   - o c) Set
   - o d) String
   - o **Answer:** b) List

3. **Which method is used to add a new item to a list in Python?**
   - o a) `append()`
   - o b) `add()`
   - o c) `insert()`
   - o d) Both a and c
   - o **Answer:** d) Both a and c

4. **Which of the following methods can be used to retrieve a value from a dictionary based on its key?**
   - o a) `get()`
   - o b) `retrieve()`
   - o c) `index()`
   - o d) `find()`
   - o **Answer:** a) `get()`

5. **What is the output of the following code?**

```
class Student:
    def __init__(self, name):
        self.name = name
        self.subjects = []
    def add_subject(self, subject):
        self.subjects.append(subject)
    def get_subjects(self):
        return self.subjects

student = Student("John")
student.add_subject("Math")
student.add_subject("Science")
print(student.get_subjects())
```

   - o a) `[]`
   - o b) `['Math', 'Science']`
   - o c) `['Math', 'Science', 'Math']`

- d) None
- **Answer:** b) `['Math', 'Science']`

6. **Which data type is best used to store a collection of unique items in Python?**
    - a) List
    - b) Tuple
    - c) Set
    - d) Dictionary
    - **Answer:** c) Set

7. **Which of the following statements about tuples is true?**
    - a) Tuples are mutable.
    - b) Tuples can store items of different data types.
    - c) Tuples are ideal for use cases where the collection of items may change over time.
    - d) Tuples have a `remove()` method.
    - **Answer:** b) Tuples can store items of different data types.

8. **In Python, how do you define a dictionary with key-value pairs?**
    - a) `d = [("name", "John"), ("age", 25)]`
    - b) `d = {"name": "John", "age": 25}`
    - c) `d = ("name" -> "John", "age" -> 25)`
    - d) `d = dict["name": "John", "age": 25]`
    - **Answer:** b) `d = {"name": "John", "age": 25}`

9. **Which method in the dictionary class allows you to add a new key-value pair?**
    - a) `add()`
    - b) `insert()`
    - c) `update()`
    - d) `append()`
    - **Answer:** c) `update()`

10. **What is the primary difference between a list and a tuple?**
    - a) A list is ordered, and a tuple is unordered.
    - b) A list is mutable, and a tuple is immutable.
    - c) A list is more efficient than a tuple.
    - d) A list can store only numbers, while a tuple can store any type of data.
    - **Answer:** b) A list is mutable, and a tuple is immutable.

Iterating Through Objects (iter and next)

11. **Which of the following is required to make an object iterable in Python?**
    - a) Implementing `__iter__` method
    - b) Implementing `__next__` method
    - c) Both `__iter__` and `__next__` methods
    - d) Using the `iter()` function
    - **Answer:** c) Both `__iter__` and `__next__` methods

12. **Which of the following is raised when there are no more items to iterate over in a Python iterator?**
    - o a) `StopIteration`
    - o b) `IndexError`
    - o c) `EndOfList`
    - o d) `IteratorException`
    - o **Answer:** a) `StopIteration`

13. **What does the `__next__` method in an iterator do?**
    - o a) Returns the current item
    - o b) Returns the next item in the sequence
    - o c) Starts the iteration process
    - o d) Resets the iterator
    - o **Answer:** b) Returns the next item in the sequence

14. **In the `__iter__` method, what should it return?**
    - o a) A list
    - o b) An iterator object
    - o c) A sequence of values
    - o d) A function that generates values
    - o **Answer:** b) An iterator object

15. **What is the output of the following code?**

```python
class Reverse:
    def __init__(self, data):
        self.data = data
        self.index = len(data)

    def __iter__(self):
        return self

    def __next__(self):
        if self.index == 0:
            raise StopIteration
        self.index -= 1
        return self.data[self.index]

rev = Reverse("Python")
for char in rev:
    print(char, end=" ")
```

    - o a) P y t h o n
    - o b) n o h t y P
    - o c) Python
    - o d) Error
    - o **Answer:** b) n o h t y P

16. **Which of the following methods is used to make an object of a class iterable?**
    - o a) `__iter__`
    - o b) `__next__`
    - o c) `next()`
    - o d) `__iter__` and `__next__`
    - o **Answer:** d) `__iter__` and `__next__`

17. **Which of the following is the correct way to define an iterator in Python?**
    - o a) Define `__next__` method only.
    - o b) Define `__iter__` and `__next__` methods.
    - o c) Use `for` loop with `__iter__`.
    - o d) Define `__iter__` method only.
    - o **Answer:** b) Define `__iter__` and `__next__` methods.
18. **How does the `__next__` method indicate the end of an iteration?**
    - o a) By returning `None`
    - o b) By raising a `StopIteration` exception
    - o c) By returning `False`
    - o d) By resetting the index
    - o **Answer:** b) By raising a `StopIteration` exception
19. **What is the default behavior if `__next__` is not defined in a custom iterator?**
    - o a) It will raise an `AttributeError`
    - o b) The `StopIteration` exception is raised automatically
    - o c) It will return `None`
    - o d) It will repeat the iteration indefinitely
    - o **Answer:** a) It will raise an `AttributeError`
20. **In the context of an iterator, which method should be called to retrieve the next item from the collection?**
    - o a) `next()`
    - o b) `__iter__()`
    - o c) `get_next()`
    - o d) `fetch()`
    - o **Answer:** a) `next()`

Practical Examples

21. **What is the output of the following code?**

```
class TodoList:
    def __init__(self):
        self.tasks = []
    def add_task(self, task):
        self.tasks.append(task)
    def __iter__(self):
        return iter(self.tasks)

todo = TodoList()
todo.add_task("Complete homework")
todo.add_task("Read book")
for task in todo:
    print(task)
```

   - o a) Complete homework Read book
   - o b) Complete homework
   - o c) Read book

- o d) Error
- o **Answer:** a) Complete homework Read book

22. **In the `StudentGrades` class, what would happen if you try to access a non-existing grade?**
   - o a) It will raise a `KeyError`
   - o b) It will return `None`
   - o c) It will return "No grade available"
   - o d) It will return an empty dictionary
   - o **Answer:** c) It will return "No grade available"

23. **What is the output of the following code?**

```python
class Employee:
    def __init__(self, name):
        self.name = name
        self.salary_details = {}
    def add_salary(self, month, salary):
        self.salary_details[month] = salary
    def get_salary(self, month):
        return self.salary_details.get(month, "No record")

emp = Employee("John")
emp.add_salary("January", 5000)
print(emp.get_salary("January"))
print(emp.get_salary("February"))
```

   - o a) 5000 No record
   - o b) January No record
   - o c) 5000 0
   - o d) Error
   - o **Answer:** a) 5000 No record

24. **Which Python method is used to check if a key exists in a dictionary inside a class?**
   - o a) `exists()`
   - o b) `contains()`
   - o c) `has_key()`
   - o d) `in`
   - o **Answer:** d) `in`

25. **What is the output of the following code?**

```python
class Counter:
    def __init__(self, start=0):
        self.count = start
    def __iter__(self):
        return self
    def __next__(self):
        self.count += 1
        return self.count

counter = Counter()
for _ in range(3):
    print(next(counter))
```

- a) 1 2 3
- b) 0 1 2
- c) 1 2 3 4
- d) 0 1 2 3
- **Answer:** a) 1 2 3

Conclusion

In this chapter, we've discussed how to manage collections like lists, tuples, and dictionaries within classes. These collections are used to store and manipulate data efficiently in object-oriented programs. We also learned how to make classes iterable by implementing the __iter__ and __next__ methods, allowing objects to be used in `for` loops. Finally, we saw practical examples of using these techniques to manage real-world data structures such as libraries and student grades. These concepts are fundamental for creating complex, organized programs that manage multiple pieces of data in a clean and efficient manner.

CHAPTER 9: ADVANCED OOP CONCEPTS (OPTIONAL)

1. Understanding MetaClasses

What are Metaclasses?

In Python, **metaclasses** are classes that define the behavior of other classes. Just as a **class** defines the structure and behavior of its instances (objects), a **metaclass** defines the structure and behavior of classes themselves. They act as the blueprint for creating classes, allowing you to customize how classes are constructed and how they behave.

Metaclasses are an advanced feature and can be used to control class creation, modify class attributes, and even restrict or enforce certain rules regarding class instantiation. When you create a new class in Python, the class is created using a metaclass, and by default, Python uses `type` as the metaclass for all classes.

Why Metaclasses Are Useful:

- **Class Customization:** You can alter the creation of classes by defining custom behaviors for class attributes, methods, or even the class itself.
- **Enforcing Standards:** Metaclasses allow you to enforce coding standards, such as naming conventions or required attributes or methods.
- **Dynamic Modifications:** You can dynamically add or modify attributes and methods to classes at the time of their creation.

How Metaclasses Work:

When you create a class in Python, the **class itself** is an instance of a **metaclass**. The metaclass dictates how the class should be created, defined, and modified.

For instance, if you define a class `MyClass`, Python will use `type` (the default metaclass) to construct this class. However, you can specify your own custom metaclasses to define how the class is created or modify its behavior.

Metaclass Syntax:

A **metaclass** is a subclass of the `type` class. It typically overrides the `__new__` and `__init__` methods to customize class creation and initialization.

Here's a basic syntax for defining and using a metaclass:

```
class MyMeta(type):  # Define the metaclass
    def __new__(cls, name, bases, dct):
        # Customize the class creation process here
        return super().__new__(cls, name, bases, dct)
```

```
class MyClass(metaclass=MyMeta):   # Using the metaclass
    pass
```

- **MyMeta**: The custom metaclass, derived from `type`, that defines how the class `MyClass` should be created.
- **MyClass**: A class that is created using the `MyMeta` metaclass.

Example of a Metaclass:

A common use case of metaclasses is modifying class attributes during class creation. Here's an example that modifies the attribute names of a class to be in **uppercase**:

```
class UppercaseMeta(type):
    def __new__(cls, name, bases, dct):
        # Convert all attribute names to uppercase
        uppercase_attributes = {
            key.upper(): value for key, value in dct.items()
        }
        return super().__new__(cls, name, bases, uppercase_attributes)

class MyClass(metaclass=UppercaseMeta):
    lowercase = "This will be uppercase"
    another_attribute = "This too"

# Access the class attributes
print(MyClass.LOWERCASE)   # Output: This will be uppercase
print(MyClass.ANOTHER_ATTRIBUTE)   # Output: This too
```

Explanation of Example:

- **UppercaseMeta** is a custom metaclass that overrides the __new__ method to convert all attribute names of the class to uppercase during class creation.
- When `MyClass` is defined, its attribute names (`lowercase` and `another_attribute`) are automatically converted to uppercase (`LOWERCASE` and `ANOTHER_ATTRIBUTE`).
- The print statements show that the class attributes are now in uppercase.

Use Cases for Metaclasses:

Metaclasses offer powerful functionality and can be used for various purposes in object-oriented programming:

1. **Validation:**

- Ensure that certain properties or methods are present in the class when it is created. This can be useful in large systems where consistent standards need to be enforced across multiple classes.
- Example: A metaclass could be used to ensure that every class contains a specific method (e.g., __init__ or validate()).

```
class EnsureInitMeta(type):
    def __new__(cls, name, bases, dct):
        if '__init__' not in dct:
            raise TypeError(f"{name} must have an __init__
method")
        return super().__new__(cls, name, bases, dct)

class MyClass(metaclass=EnsureInitMeta):
    def __init__(self):
        pass  # Required __init__ method

# This will raise an error
class MyOtherClass(metaclass=EnsureInitMeta):
    pass  # No __init__ method defined
```

2. **Class Modification:**
   - You can dynamically add, modify, or delete class attributes or methods at the time of class creation. This allows for more flexible designs and the ability to apply reusable functionality across classes.
   - Example: Automatically add a __str__ method to classes using a metaclass.

```
class AddStrMethodMeta(type):
    def __new__(cls, name, bases, dct):
        if '__str__' not in dct:
            dct['__str__'] = lambda self:
f'{self.__class__.__name__} instance'
        return super().__new__(cls, name, bases, dct)

class MyClass(metaclass=AddStrMethodMeta):
    pass

obj = MyClass()
print(str(obj))   # Output: MyClass instance
```

3. **Singleton Pattern:**
   - The **Singleton Pattern** ensures that only one instance of a class is created. Metaclasses are often used to enforce this behavior in a clean and simple way.
   - Example: Enforce a singleton pattern to ensure that only one instance of a class is instantiated:

```
class SingletonMeta(type):
    _instances = {}

    def __call__(cls, *args, **kwargs):
        if cls not in cls._instances:
            cls._instances[cls] = super().__call__(*args,
**kwargs)
```

```
        return cls._instances[cls]

class SingletonClass(metaclass=SingletonMeta):
    pass

obj1 = SingletonClass()
obj2 = SingletonClass()

print(obj1 is obj2)  # Output: True (both are the same instance)
```

- o The `SingletonMeta` metaclass ensures that only one instance of `SingletonClass` is created, no matter how many times the class is instantiated.

.

2. Decorators in OOP

In Python, **decorators** are a powerful and flexible tool used to modify or enhance the behavior of functions or methods without changing their actual code. A decorator is essentially a **function** that takes another function (or method) as an argument, enhances or alters it, and returns a modified version of that function. This allows you to add functionality to existing functions or methods dynamically.

Decorators are widely used in Python for various purposes such as:

- **Logging**: Automatically logging function calls.
- **Access control**: Implementing authentication or authorization checks.
- **Caching/Memoization**: Storing results to improve performance.
- **Validation**: Checking function arguments before execution.

Decorators are particularly useful in **Object-Oriented Programming (OOP)** because they can be applied to methods within a class to modify their behavior without changing the class's original implementation.

How Decorators Work:

In Python, decorators are applied using the `@decorator_name` syntax, just before the function or method definition. This makes it simple to apply a decorator and modify the behavior of functions or methods.

Basic Function Decorator:

Let's start with a basic example of how a function decorator works:

```
def decorator_function(func):
    def wrapper():
        print("Before the function is called")
        func()  # Call the original function
        print("After the function is called")
    return wrapper

@decorator_function  # Apply the decorator to this function
def my_function():
    print("Function is called.")

my_function()
```

Output:

```
Before the function is called
Function is called.
After the function is called
```

Explanation of Basic Decorator:

- The `decorator_function` takes a function `func` as an argument.
- Inside `decorator_function`, we define the `wrapper` function, which calls the original `func` while adding some behavior before and after calling the function.
- `@decorator_function` is the decorator syntax that applies the `decorator_function` to `my_function`.
- When `my_function()` is called, it's actually the `wrapper()` function that runs, adding the "before" and "after" print statements around the call to the original `my_function`.

Method Decorators in Classes:

In OOP, decorators are often used to modify or enhance methods within a class. These decorators can add functionality like logging, authentication checks, and more.

Example: Logging Method Calls

Here's how decorators can be used to log method calls in a class:

```
def log_method_call(method):
    def wrapper(self, *args, **kwargs):
        print(f"Calling method {method.__name__} with arguments {args}
and keyword arguments {kwargs}")
        result = method(self, *args, **kwargs)
        print(f"Method {method.__name__} returned {result}")
        return result
    return wrapper

class Calculator:
    @log_method_call  # Decorator applied to the method
```

```
    def add(self, x, y):
        return x + y

    @log_method_call  # Decorator applied to the method
    def subtract(self, x, y):
        return x - y

# Using the Calculator class
calc = Calculator()
calc.add(2, 3)  # Logs method call and return value
calc.subtract(5, 3)  # Logs method call and return value
```

Output:

```
Calling method add with arguments (2, 3) and keyword arguments {}
Method add returned 5
Calling method subtract with arguments (5, 3) and keyword arguments {}
Method subtract returned 2
```

Explanation:

- The `log_method_call` decorator is designed to log the method name, its arguments, and the return value.
- It wraps both the `add` and `subtract` methods in the `Calculator` class.
- When the methods are called, the decorator prints out useful information like the method name, its arguments, and the returned result.

Common Use Cases for Decorators in OOP:

1. **Logging:**
   - **Use Case:** Automatically log method calls and their results for debugging or auditing purposes.
   - **Example:** A decorator that logs the method name, arguments, and result, as demonstrated above.
2. **Access Control (Authentication/Authorization):**
   - **Use Case:** Ensure that a method can only be executed by users with certain permissions or after authentication.
   - **Example:** A decorator that checks if a user is authenticated before allowing access to a certain method:

```
def authenticate_user(method):
    def wrapper(self, *args, **kwargs):
        if not self.is_authenticated:
            raise PermissionError("User not authenticated")
        return method(self, *args, **kwargs)
    return wrapper

class User:
    def __init__(self, authenticated=False):
```

```python
        self.is_authenticated = authenticated

    @authenticate_user
    def view_dashboard(self):
        return "Welcome to your dashboard!"

user = User(authenticated=True)
print(user.view_dashboard())   # Works fine

unauth_user = User(authenticated=False)
print(unauth_user.view_dashboard())   # Raises PermissionError
```

3. **Memoization (Caching):**
   o **Use Case:** Store the results of expensive function calls to improve performance by avoiding repeated calculations.
   o **Example:** A decorator that caches the result of a method based on its arguments:

```python
def memoize(func):
    cache = {}
    def wrapper(*args):
        if args in cache:
            return cache[args]
        result = func(*args)
        cache[args] = result
        return result
    return wrapper

class MathOperations:
    @memoize
    def fibonacci(self, n):
        if n <= 1:
            return n
        return self.fibonacci(n-1) + self.fibonacci(n-2)

math_ops = MathOperations()
print(math_ops.fibonacci(30))   # This call will be cached for
future use
```

4. **Validation:**
   o **Use Case:** Check arguments before executing a method to ensure they are valid (e.g., type checking or range validation).
   o **Example:** A decorator that validates if the arguments of a method are within a certain range:

```python
def validate_positive_args(method):
    def wrapper(self, *args, **kwargs):
        if any(arg <= 0 for arg in args):
            raise ValueError("Arguments must be positive")
        return method(self, *args, **kwargs)
    return wrapper

class BankAccount:
    @validate_positive_args
```

```
    def deposit(self, amount):
        print(f"Deposited {amount} into account")

account = BankAccount()
account.deposit(100)   # Works fine
account.deposit(-50)   # Raises ValueError
```

3. Introduction to Design Patterns (Singleton, Factory)

Design patterns are general solutions to recurring design problems that developers face when writing code. They represent best practices for solving specific challenges in software design and provide templates that can be reused in different scenarios. In Object-Oriented Programming (OOP), design patterns help structure your code in a way that is maintainable, scalable, and flexible.

Two of the most commonly used design patterns are **Singleton** and **Factory**. These patterns address different concerns:

- **Singleton Pattern**: Ensures that a class has only one instance and provides a global point of access to that instance.
- **Factory Pattern**: Provides an interface for creating objects, without specifying their exact class, allowing for more flexibility and decoupling of object creation logic.

Let's dive into each of these patterns in detail.

Singleton Pattern

The **Singleton Pattern** ensures that a class has only **one instance** throughout the entire system. This pattern is useful when you need to control access to shared resources such as a database connection or a configuration manager. By ensuring a single instance, it helps in managing resources efficiently and avoids the overhead of creating multiple instances of the same class.

How the Singleton Pattern Works:

- The **Singleton pattern** restricts the instantiation of a class to just **one object**.
- It uses a static variable (often called _instance) to store the single instance of the class.
- A special method (commonly __new__ in Python) is used to control object creation. The method ensures that only the first instantiation creates the object, and subsequent instantiations return the same object.

Example:

```
class Singleton:
    _instance = None   # Class variable to hold the single instance

    def __new__(cls):
        if cls._instance is None:   # Check if an instance already
exists
            cls._instance = super(Singleton, cls).__new__(cls)   #
Create the instance if it doesn't exist
        return cls._instance   # Return the same instance every time

# Using Singleton
obj1 = Singleton()
obj2 = Singleton()

print(obj1 is obj2)   # Output: True (both refer to the same instance)
```

Explanation:

- The `__new__` method in the `Singleton` class checks if the `_instance` variable is `None`. If it is, it creates a new instance using `super(Singleton, cls).__new__(cls)`.
- For subsequent instantiations, it simply returns the existing instance, ensuring that only one instance of the class exists.
- In the example, `obj1` and `obj2` will be the same object (`obj1 is obj2` will return `True`).

Use Cases:

- **Database Connections**: Ensure that only one instance of a database connection exists throughout the application.
- **Configuration Settings**: Store and access global configurations or settings, avoiding multiple objects holding different states.
- **Logging Systems**: A single logger instance can be shared across different parts of the application for consistency.

Factory Pattern

The **Factory Pattern** is a **creational design pattern** that defines an interface for creating objects, but allows subclasses to alter the type of objects that will be created. It is particularly useful when the client doesn't need to know about the exact type of the object it is working with, just that it can use a factory to get the right object based on specific input or conditions.

How the Factory Pattern Works:

- The **Factory Method** provides a way to create objects, but the object creation logic is hidden from the client code.
- Instead of directly creating objects using the `new` keyword, the client uses a factory method, which decides what type of object to instantiate based on input parameters.

Example:

```
class Dog:
    def speak(self):
        return "Woof!"  # Dog's sound

class Cat:
    def speak(self):
        return "Meow!"  # Cat's sound

class AnimalFactory:
    def get_animal(self, animal_type):
        if animal_type == "dog":
            return Dog()  # Returns a Dog object
        elif animal_type == "cat":
            return Cat()  # Returns a Cat object
        else:
            return None  # Unknown animal type

# Using the Factory
factory = AnimalFactory()

animal = factory.get_animal("dog")
print(animal.speak())  # Output: Woof!

animal = factory.get_animal("cat")
print(animal.speak())  # Output: Meow!
```

Explanation:

- The `AnimalFactory` class provides a method `get_animal` that takes a string (`animal_type`) as input and returns the corresponding animal object (`Dog` or `Cat`).
- The client code does not need to know about the exact class (e.g., `Dog` or `Cat`) that is being created. It simply calls the `get_animal` method with the type of animal it needs, and the factory decides how to create the object.
- This abstracts away the object creation process, making the code more flexible and decoupled.

Use Cases:

- **Creating Complex Objects**: When the object creation involves complex logic or a lot of setup (e.g., setting up parameters, creating multiple sub-objects), the Factory pattern can centralize and manage this process.
- **Frameworks and Libraries**: Frameworks often use factories to abstract away the exact class being instantiated, providing a cleaner interface for users.

- **GUI Frameworks**: In GUI frameworks, you may need to create different types of UI components (buttons, labels, text fields, etc.). The Factory pattern can dynamically create these components based on user input or configurations.

1. Practical Examples on Advanced OOP Concepts

Example 1: Understanding MetaClasses

```
# A basic metaclass example that alters class creation
class MetaClass(type):
    def __new__(cls, name, bases, class_dict):
        class_dict['class_type'] = 'MetaClass Example'
        return super(MetaClass, cls).__new__(cls, name, bases,
class_dict)

class MyClass(metaclass=MetaClass):
    pass

# Creating an instance of MyClass
obj = MyClass()
print(obj.class_type)   # Output: MetaClass Example
```

Explanation: A metaclass controls the creation of classes. In this example, the metaclass `MetaClass` adds a `class_type` attribute to any class that uses it as the metaclass.

Example 2: MetaClass with Custom Behavior

```
# Metaclass that ensures all class names are uppercase
class UpperCaseMeta(type):
    def __new__(cls, name, bases, class_dict):
        name = name.upper()
        return super(UpperCaseMeta, cls).__new__(cls, name, bases,
class_dict)

class MyClass(metaclass=UpperCaseMeta):
    pass

print(MyClass.__name__)   # Output: MYCLASS
```

Explanation: Here, `UpperCaseMeta` ensures that the name of the class being created is always in uppercase.

Example 3: Decorators for Logging Method Calls

```
def log_method_call(method):
```

```
    def wrapper(self, *args, **kwargs):
        print(f"Calling method {method.__name__} with args {args} and
kwargs {kwargs}")
        result = method(self, *args, **kwargs)
        print(f"Method {method.__name__} returned {result}")
        return result
    return wrapper

class Calculator:
    @log_method_call
    def add(self, x, y):
        return x + y

calc = Calculator()
calc.add(5, 10)
```

Explanation: A decorator is used to log the arguments and return values of methods in the `Calculator` class.

Example 4: MetaClass for Class Validation

```
class ValidationMeta(type):
    def __new__(cls, name, bases, class_dict):
        if 'validate' not in class_dict:
            raise TypeError(f"Class {name} must implement a validate
method")
        return super(ValidationMeta, cls).__new__(cls, name, bases,
class_dict)

class User(metaclass=ValidationMeta):
    def validate(self):
        return True

# This will raise an error as validate is not implemented
# class Product(metaclass=ValidationMeta):
#     pass
```

Explanation: `ValidationMeta` ensures that any class using it must implement a `validate` method.

Example 5: Singleton Pattern for Database Connection

```
class DatabaseConnection:
    _instance = None

    def __new__(cls):
        if cls._instance is None:
            cls._instance = super(DatabaseConnection, cls).__new__(cls)
```

```
            cls._instance.connection = "Database Connection
Established"
        return cls._instance

db1 = DatabaseConnection()
db2 = DatabaseConnection()

print(db1 is db2)  # Output: True (both refer to the same instance)
```

Explanation: The `DatabaseConnection` class ensures only one instance exists, sharing the same connection.

Example 6: Factory Pattern to Create Animal Objects

```
class Dog:
    def speak(self):
        return "Woof!"

class Cat:
    def speak(self):
        return "Meow!"

class AnimalFactory:
    def get_animal(self, animal_type):
        if animal_type == "dog":
            return Dog()
        elif animal_type == "cat":
            return Cat()

factory = AnimalFactory()
animal = factory.get_animal("dog")
print(animal.speak())  # Output: Woof!
```

Explanation: `AnimalFactory` provides a way to create different animal objects based on the input.

Example 7: Singleton Pattern for Logger

```
class Logger:
    _instance = None

    def __new__(cls):
        if cls._instance is None:
            cls._instance = super(Logger, cls).__new__(cls)
            cls._instance.logs = []
        return cls._instance

    def log(self, message):
        self.logs.append(message)
```

```
logger1 = Logger()
logger1.log("First log entry")

logger2 = Logger()
logger2.log("Second log entry")

print(logger1.logs)  # Output: ['First log entry', 'Second log entry']
```

Explanation: The Logger class ensures a single logger instance throughout the application.

Example 8: Factory Pattern for Car Creation

```
class Sedan:
    def type(self):
        return "Sedan"

class SUV:
    def type(self):
        return "SUV"

class CarFactory:
    def get_car(self, car_type):
        if car_type == "sedan":
            return Sedan()
        elif car_type == "suv":
            return SUV()

factory = CarFactory()
car = factory.get_car("sedan")
print(car.type())  # Output: Sedan
```

Explanation: The CarFactory creates either a Sedan or SUV object based on the input.

Example 9: Decorator for Caching Method Results

```
def cache_result(method):
    cache = {}

    def wrapper(self, *args, **kwargs):
        if args in cache:
            return cache[args]
        result = method(self, *args, **kwargs)
        cache[args] = result
        return result

    return wrapper
```

```
class MathOperations:
    @cache_result
    def add(self, x, y):
        return x + y

math = MathOperations()
print(math.add(2, 3))   # Computes and caches result
print(math.add(2, 3))   # Returns cached result
```

Explanation: This decorator caches the result of the method `add` so that repeated calls with the same arguments return the cached result.

Example 10: Using MetaClass to Create a Singleton Class

```
class SingletonMeta(type):
    _instances = {}

    def __call__(cls, *args, **kwargs):
        if cls not in cls._instances:
            instance = super().__call__(*args, **kwargs)
            cls._instances[cls] = instance
        return cls._instances[cls]

class MySingleton(metaclass=SingletonMeta):
    def __init__(self):
        self.value = 42

# Creating instances
obj1 = MySingleton()
obj2 = MySingleton()

print(obj1 is obj2)   # Output: True (both refer to the same instance)
```

Explanation: The `SingletonMeta` metaclass ensures only one instance of `MySingleton` exists.

2. Multiple Choice Questions (MCQs)

1. **What is the main purpose of a metaclass in Python?**
   - o   A) To create multiple instances of a class
   - o   B) To define the behavior of a class at runtime
   - o   C) To add additional attributes to an object
   - o   D) To define object initialization

   Answer: B

2. **Which of the following is true about the Singleton pattern?**
   - ○ A) It ensures that a class has multiple instances
   - ○ B) It is used to create new instances of a class at will
   - ○ C) It restricts the instantiation of a class to a single object
   - ○ D) It guarantees that classes cannot be inherited

   Answer: C

3. **Which of the following decorators can be used to modify the behavior of a method?**
   - ○ A) @staticmethod
   - ○ B) @classmethod
   - ○ C) @log_method_call
   - ○ D) @property

   Answer: C

4. **In the Factory pattern, what is the role of the factory method?**
   - ○ A) To create only one instance of an object
   - ○ B) To instantiate an object based on input
   - ○ C) To define class attributes
   - ○ D) To manage object relationships

   Answer: B

5. **Which metaclass allows for enforcing a class name to be in uppercase?**
   - ○ A) SingletonMeta
   - ○ B) UpperCaseMeta
   - ○ C) FactoryMeta
   - ○ D) ValidationMeta

   Answer: B

6. **What will be the result of `obj1 is obj2` if both `obj1` and `obj2` are instances of a Singleton class?**
   - ○ A) False
   - ○ B) True
   - ○ C) None
   - ○ D) It will raise an exception

   Answer: B

7. **In the context of decorators, what does the `wrapper` function do?**
   - o A) It defines the arguments for the decorated method
   - o B) It adds logging functionality to the method
   - o C) It wraps the original function with additional behavior
   - o D) It replaces the original method entirely

   Answer: C

8. **Which of the following is the correct way to define a metaclass?**
   - o A) `class MyClass(metaclass=MyMetaClass):`
   - o B) `class MyClass(meta=MyMetaClass):`
   - o C) `class MyClass(meta=MyMeta()):`
   - o D) `class MyClass(metaclass=MyMeta()):`

   Answer: A

9. **Which of the following patterns provides an interface for creating objects without specifying their exact class?**
   - o A) Singleton Pattern
   - o B) Factory Pattern
   - o C) Observer Pattern
   - o D) Strategy Pattern

   Answer: B

10. **What does the `__new__` method do in a Singleton pattern?**
    - o A) It creates the initial instance of a class
    - o B) It overrides the default initialization method
    - o C) It ensures that only one instance of the class is created
    - o D) It initializes the class attributes

    Answer: C

11. **Which design pattern ensures that only one instance of a class exists?**
    - o A) Factory Pattern
    - o B) Singleton Pattern
    - o C) Strategy Pattern
    - o D) Observer Pattern

    Answer: B

12. **Which decorator can be used to log method calls and return values?**
    - o A) @staticmethod
    - o B) @classmethod
    - o C) @log_method_call
    - o D) @property

Answer: C

13. **In the Factory pattern, which class is responsible for creating objects?**
    - ○ A) Product class
    - ○ B) Factory class
    - ○ C) Abstract class
    - ○ D) Client class

Answer: B

14. **Which of the following is a key benefit of the Singleton pattern?**
    - ○ A) It allows for multiple instances of a class to exist
    - ○ B) It helps in sharing resources globally
    - ○ C) It is used for logging purposes
    - ○ D) It enforces class inheritance

Answer: B

15. **Which decorator is used for caching method results in Python?**
    - ○ A) @staticmethod
    - ○ B) @lru_cache
    - ○ C) @property
    - ○ D) @log_method_call

Answer: B

16. **In a factory pattern, what is the relationship between the factory class and product classes?**
    - ○ A) Factory class inherits product classes
    - ○ B) Factory class creates product objects
    - ○ C) Product classes create the factory
    - ○ D) There is no relationship

Answer: B

17. **What will happen if the Singleton pattern is violated?**
    - ○ A) Multiple instances will be created
    - ○ B) The program will crash
    - ○ C) The instance will not have any attributes
    - ○ D) It will automatically reinitialize

Answer: A

18. **Which design pattern is typically used for object creation when the system needs to be flexible in which type of object is created?**
    - ○ A) Observer Pattern
    - ○ B) Singleton Pattern

o C) Factory Pattern
o D) Proxy Pattern

Answer: C

19. **What is the primary function of the __call__ method in a metaclass?**
    o A) To initialize an object
    o B) To control instance creation
    o C) To define class attributes
    o D) To manage method overriding

Answer: B

20. **Which of the following is true about a decorator?**
    o A) It can modify the behavior of a class
    o B) It can be applied to any function or method
    o C) It is a subclass of the original method
    o D) It is a type of metaclass

Answer: B

21. **Which of the following patterns is not related to object creation?**
    o A) Singleton Pattern
    o B) Factory Pattern
    o C) Observer Pattern
    o D) Abstract Factory Pattern

Answer: C

22. **What does the term "duck typing" refer to in Python?**
    o A) Static typing of objects
    o B) Object type is determined at runtime
    o C) Ensuring an object follows a specific interface
    o D) Both B and C

Answer: D

23. **Which method is used to define a class's behavior in a metaclass?**
    o A) __new__
    o B) __call__
    o C) __init__
    o D) __setattr__

Answer: A

24. What does the `log_method_call` decorator do?
   - ○ A) It returns the function without modification
   - ○ B) It adds logging functionality to methods
   - ○ C) It limits method execution to one call
   - ○ D) It modifies method parameters

Answer: B

25. Which of the following is an advantage of using decorators in Python?
   - ○ A) It allows adding functionality without modifying the original code
   - ○ B) It restricts inheritance in classes
   - ○ C) It improves execution speed
   - ○ D) It simplifies code by reducing function arguments

Answer: A

Conclusion

The advanced OOP concepts covered in this chapter—**Metaclasses, Decorators**, and **Design Patterns**—are powerful tools that can be used to create more flexible, maintainable, and scalable software. While these topics might not be needed for every project, understanding and applying them appropriately can significantly enhance your ability to design complex systems efficiently. By mastering these advanced techniques, you can improve the quality of your OOP designs and take your programming skills to the next level.

APPENDICES

APPENDIX A: PYTHON OOP INTERVIEW QUESTIONS

IN THIS SECTION, WE WILL LOOK AT SOME OF THE MOST COMMONLY ASKED OBJECT-ORIENTED PROGRAMMING (OOP) INTERVIEW QUESTIONS FOR PYTHON. THESE QUESTIONS ARE DESIGNED TO ASSESS YOUR UNDERSTANDING OF THE CORE CONCEPTS OF OOP, WHICH ARE ENCAPSULATION, INHERITANCE, POLYMORPHISM, AND ABSTRACTION.

- **WHAT IS OBJECT-ORIENTED PROGRAMMING (OOP)?**

  - **EXPLANATION:** OOP IS A PROGRAMMING PARADIGM THAT ORGANIZES SOFTWARE DESIGN AROUND DATA (OBJECTS) RATHER THAN FUNCTIONS. IT FOCUSES ON THE CREATION OF CLASSES AND OBJECTS THAT ENCAPSULATE DATA AND BEHAVIOR. THE FOUR PILLARS OF OOP ARE ENCAPSULATION, INHERITANCE, POLYMORPHISM, AND ABSTRACTION.

- **WHAT IS A CLASS IN PYTHON?**

  - **EXPLANATION:** A CLASS IN PYTHON IS A BLUEPRINT FOR CREATING OBJECTS. IT DEFINES THE ATTRIBUTES (VARIABLES) AND METHODS (FUNCTIONS) THAT ARE SHARED BY ALL OBJECTS OF THAT CLASS.

- **WHAT IS AN OBJECT IN PYTHON?**

  - **EXPLANATION:** AN OBJECT IS AN INSTANCE OF A CLASS. IT REPRESENTS A REAL-WORLD ENTITY AND IS CREATED BASED ON THE CLASS BLUEPRINT. AN OBJECT CONTAINS DATA (ATTRIBUTES) AND METHODS THAT OPERATE ON THAT DATA.

- **WHAT IS THE SELF KEYWORD IN PYTHON?**

  - **EXPLANATION:** THE SELF KEYWORD REFERS TO THE INSTANCE OF THE CLASS. IT IS USED TO ACCESS THE ATTRIBUTES AND METHODS OF THE CURRENT OBJECT.

- **EXPLAIN THE CONCEPT OF ENCAPSULATION IN PYTHON.**

  - **EXPLANATION:** ENCAPSULATION IS THE BUNDLING OF DATA AND METHODS THAT OPERATE ON THAT DATA WITHIN A SINGLE UNIT, I.E., A

CLASS. IT HELPS IN HIDING THE INTERNAL STATE OF THE OBJECT AND EXPOSING ONLY NECESSARY FUNCTIONALITY VIA METHODS.

- **WHAT IS THE DIFFERENCE BETWEEN A CLASS METHOD AND AN INSTANCE METHOD?**

  - **EXPLANATION:** AN INSTANCE METHOD TAKES SELF AS THE FIRST PARAMETER, WHICH REFERS TO THE INSTANCE OF THE CLASS. A CLASS METHOD TAKES CLS AS THE FIRST PARAMETER, WHICH REFERS TO THE CLASS ITSELF. CLASS METHODS CAN ACCESS AND MODIFY CLASS-LEVEL ATTRIBUTES.

- **WHAT IS INHERITANCE IN PYTHON?**

  - **EXPLANATION:** INHERITANCE IS A MECHANISM IN PYTHON THAT ALLOWS A CLASS TO INHERIT ATTRIBUTES AND METHODS FROM ANOTHER CLASS, ENABLING CODE REUSE AND THE CREATION OF HIERARCHICAL RELATIONSHIPS BETWEEN CLASSES.

- **WHAT IS METHOD OVERRIDING IN PYTHON?**

  - **EXPLANATION:** METHOD OVERRIDING OCCURS WHEN A SUBCLASS DEFINES A METHOD THAT ALREADY EXISTS IN ITS SUPERCLASS, PROVIDING ITS OWN IMPLEMENTATION.

- **WHAT IS POLYMORPHISM IN PYTHON?**

  - **EXPLANATION:** POLYMORPHISM ALLOWS METHODS TO BEHAVE DIFFERENTLY BASED ON THE OBJECT CALLING THEM. IT CAN BE ACHIEVED VIA METHOD OVERRIDING OR METHOD OVERLOADING.

- **WHAT IS THE DIFFERENCE BETWEEN @STATICMETHOD AND @CLASSMETHOD IN PYTHON?**

  - **EXPLANATION:**
    - @STATICMETHOD: A METHOD THAT DOES NOT TAKE SELF OR CLS AS THE FIRST ARGUMENT. IT BEHAVES LIKE A REGULAR FUNCTION THAT BELONGS TO THE CLASS.
    - @CLASSMETHOD: A METHOD THAT TAKES CLS AS THE FIRST ARGUMENT AND IS USED TO MODIFY OR ACCESS CLASS-LEVEL ATTRIBUTES.

- **WHAT IS MULTIPLE INHERITANCE IN PYTHON?**

  - **EXPLANATION:** MULTIPLE INHERITANCE ALLOWS A CLASS TO INHERIT FROM MORE THAN ONE CLASS. PYTHON SUPPORTS MULTIPLE INHERITANCE, ALLOWING A CLASS TO HAVE MULTIPLE PARENT CLASSES.

- **WHAT IS A CONSTRUCTOR IN PYTHON?**

  - **EXPLANATION:** A CONSTRUCTOR IS A SPECIAL METHOD (__INIT__) THAT IS AUTOMATICALLY CALLED WHEN A NEW OBJECT IS CREATED. IT IS USED TO INITIALIZE THE OBJECT'S ATTRIBUTES.

- **WHAT IS A DESTRUCTOR IN PYTHON?**

  - **EXPLANATION:** A DESTRUCTOR (__DEL__) IS A SPECIAL METHOD IN PYTHON THAT IS AUTOMATICALLY CALLED WHEN AN OBJECT IS DESTROYED, USUALLY WHEN IT GOES OUT OF SCOPE OR IS EXPLICITLY DELETED.

- **WHAT IS AN ABSTRACT CLASS IN PYTHON?**

  - **EXPLANATION:** AN ABSTRACT CLASS IS A CLASS THAT CANNOT BE INSTANTIATED AND MUST BE SUBCLASSED. IT CAN CONTAIN ABSTRACT METHODS, WHICH MUST BE IMPLEMENTED BY SUBCLASSES.

- **WHAT IS THE ABC MODULE IN PYTHON?**

  - **EXPLANATION:** THE ABC (ABSTRACT BASE CLASS) MODULE PROVIDES TOOLS FOR DEFINING ABSTRACT CLASSES. IT ALLOWS YOU TO DEFINE ABSTRACT METHODS THAT MUST BE IMPLEMENTED BY SUBCLASSES.

- **HOW DO YOU PREVENT A CLASS FROM BEING SUBCLASSED IN PYTHON?**

  - **EXPLANATION:** YOU CAN PREVENT A CLASS FROM BEING SUBCLASSED BY USING THE FINAL DECORATOR FROM THE TYPING MODULE (IN PYTHON 3.8+). ALTERNATIVELY, YOU CAN OVERRIDE __NEW__ TO PREVENT INSTANTIATION.

- **WHAT IS THE DIFFERENCE BETWEEN IS AND == IN PYTHON?**

  - **EXPLANATION:** IS CHECKS IF TWO VARIABLES REFER TO THE SAME OBJECT IN MEMORY, WHILE == CHECKS IF THE VALUES OF TWO VARIABLES ARE EQUAL.

- **WHAT ARE CLASS ATTRIBUTES AND INSTANCE ATTRIBUTES?**

  - **EXPLANATION:**
    - CLASS ATTRIBUTES ARE SHARED BY ALL INSTANCES OF A CLASS.
    - INSTANCE ATTRIBUTES ARE SPECIFIC TO EACH OBJECT CREATED FROM THE CLASS.

- **WHAT IS THE PURPOSE OF THE super() FUNCTION IN PYTHON?**

  - **EXPLANATION:** super() IS USED TO CALL A METHOD FROM A SUPERCLASS. IT ALLOWS YOU TO INVOKE METHODS IN THE PARENT CLASS, TYPICALLY USED FOR METHOD OVERRIDING.

- **WHAT IS THE DIFFERENCE BETWEEN A SHALLOW COPY AND A DEEP COPY IN PYTHON?**

  - **EXPLANATION:** A SHALLOW COPY CREATES A NEW OBJECT BUT DOES NOT COPY NESTED OBJECTS, JUST REFERENCES THEM. A DEEP COPY CREATES A COMPLETELY INDEPENDENT COPY OF THE ORIGINAL OBJECT, INCLUDING NESTED OBJECTS.

- **WHAT IS THE __str__ METHOD IN PYTHON?**

  - **EXPLANATION:** THE __str__ METHOD IS USED TO DEFINE A STRING REPRESENTATION OF AN OBJECT. IT IS CALLED WHEN print() IS USED ON AN OBJECT.

- **WHAT IS THE __repr__ METHOD IN PYTHON?**

  - **EXPLANATION:** THE __repr__ METHOD IS USED TO DEFINE A FORMAL STRING REPRESENTATION OF AN OBJECT, MAINLY FOR DEBUGGING. IT IS OFTEN CALLED BY THE repr() FUNCTION.

- **WHAT ARE GETATTR(), SETATTR(), AND DELATTR() IN PYTHON?**

  - **EXPLANATION:** THESE ARE BUILT-IN FUNCTIONS THAT PROVIDE DYNAMIC ACCESS TO AN OBJECT'S ATTRIBUTES:
    - GETATTR(OBJ, NAME) RETURNS THE VALUE OF THE ATTRIBUTE NAME.
    - SETATTR(OBJ, NAME, VALUE) SETS THE VALUE OF THE ATTRIBUTE NAME.
    - DELATTR(OBJ, NAME) DELETES THE ATTRIBUTE NAME.

- **WHAT IS THE DIFFERENCE BETWEEN __NEW__ AND __INIT__ IN PYTHON?**

  - **EXPLANATION:** __NEW__ IS RESPONSIBLE FOR CREATING A NEW OBJECT, WHILE __INIT__ IS USED TO INITIALIZE THE OBJECT'S STATE AFTER IT IS CREATED.

- **WHAT ARE THE ADVANTAGES OF USING OOP IN PYTHON?**

  - **EXPLANATION:** THE ADVANTAGES OF OOP IN PYTHON INCLUDE CODE REUSE (VIA INHERITANCE), MODULARITY, FLEXIBILITY (POLYMORPHISM), AND EASIER MAINTENANCE DUE TO ENCAPSULATION.

- **CAN YOU EXPLAIN HOW PYTHON SUPPORTS ENCAPSULATION?**

  - **EXPLANATION:** PYTHON SUPPORTS ENCAPSULATION BY ALLOWING CLASSES TO DEFINE PRIVATE ATTRIBUTES AND METHODS, TYPICALLY USING A SINGLE OR DOUBLE UNDERSCORE (_NAME, __NAME) TO INDICATE PRIVATE MEMBERS.

- **WHAT IS A METACLASS IN PYTHON?**

  - **EXPLANATION:** A METACLASS IS A CLASS THAT DEFINES THE BEHAVIOR OF OTHER CLASSES. IT ALLOWS YOU TO CONTROL THE CREATION AND BEHAVIOR OF CLASSES THEMSELVES.

- **HOW DO YOU CREATE A PRIVATE ATTRIBUTE IN PYTHON?**

  - **EXPLANATION:** PRIVATE ATTRIBUTES CAN BE CREATED USING A DOUBLE UNDERSCORE (__) BEFORE THE ATTRIBUTE NAME, WHICH

TRIGGERS NAME MANGLING, MAKING IT HARDER (BUT NOT IMPOSSIBLE) TO ACCESS FROM OUTSIDE THE CLASS.

- **WHAT IS METHOD RESOLUTION ORDER (MRO) IN PYTHON?**

  - **EXPLANATION:** MRO DEFINES THE ORDER IN WHICH PYTHON SEARCHES FOR METHODS IN CASE OF MULTIPLE INHERITANCE. IT FOLLOWS THE C3 LINEARIZATION ALGORITHM TO DETERMINE THE METHOD LOOKUP ORDER.

- **WHAT IS DUCK TYPING IN PYTHON?**

  - **EXPLANATION:** DUCK TYPING IS A CONCEPT WHERE THE TYPE OR CLASS OF AN OBJECT IS DETERMINED BY ITS BEHAVIOR (METHODS AND ATTRIBUTES) RATHER THAN ITS ACTUAL TYPE. "IF IT WALKS LIKE A DUCK AND QUACKS LIKE A DUCK, IT MUST BE A DUCK."

- **WHAT ARE CLASS DECORATORS IN PYTHON?**

  - **EXPLANATION:** CLASS DECORATORS ARE FUNCTIONS THAT MODIFY OR ENHANCE THE BEHAVIOR OF CLASSES. THEY ARE USED TO ADD FUNCTIONALITY TO CLASSES WITHOUT MODIFYING THEIR CODE.

- **CAN YOU EXPLAIN THE __CALL__ METHOD IN PYTHON?**

  - **EXPLANATION:** THE __CALL__ METHOD ALLOWS AN OBJECT TO BE CALLED AS A FUNCTION. IT IS USED TO DEFINE CUSTOM BEHAVIOR WHEN AN INSTANCE IS CALLED LIKE A FUNCTION.

- **WHAT IS THE DIFFERENCE BETWEEN @PROPERTY AND @STATICMETHOD IN PYTHON?**

  - **EXPLANATION:**
    - @PROPERTY IS USED TO DEFINE A METHOD AS AN ATTRIBUTE, ALLOWING YOU TO ACCESS IT LIKE A REGULAR ATTRIBUTE BUT WITH ADDITIONAL FUNCTIONALITY.
    - @STATICMETHOD IS USED TO DEFINE A METHOD THAT DOESN'T TAKE SELF OR CLS AS THE FIRST ARGUMENT.

- **WHAT IS A CLASS VARIABLE IN PYTHON?**

- **EXPLANATION:** A CLASS VARIABLE IS A VARIABLE THAT IS SHARED BY ALL INSTANCES OF A CLASS. IT IS DEFINED WITHIN THE CLASS BUT OUTSIDE ANY INSTANCE METHODS.

- **EXPLAIN THE DIFFERENCE BETWEEN IS AND == OPERATORS.**

  - **EXPLANATION:** IS CHECKS IF TWO VARIABLES POINT TO THE SAME OBJECT IN MEMORY, WHILE == CHECKS IF TWO VARIABLES HAVE THE SAME VALUE.

- **WHAT IS THE __DEL__ METHOD USED FOR IN PYTHON?**

  - **EXPLANATION:** THE __DEL__ METHOD IS A DESTRUCTOR, WHICH IS CALLED WHEN AN OBJECT IS DESTROYED. IT IS OFTEN USED TO RELEASE RESOURCES BEFORE THE OBJECT IS REMOVED FROM MEMORY.

- **WHAT IS A SINGLETON CLASS IN PYTHON?**

  - **EXPLANATION:** A SINGLETON CLASS IS DESIGNED TO ALLOW ONLY ONE INSTANCE OF THE CLASS TO BE CREATED. ANY SUBSEQUENT ATTEMPTS TO CREATE AN INSTANCE RETURN THE SAME OBJECT.

- **WHAT IS THE PURPOSE OF THE __SLOTS__ FEATURE IN PYTHON?**

  - **EXPLANATION:** THE __SLOTS__ FEATURE IS USED TO RESTRICT THE ATTRIBUTES THAT AN OBJECT CAN HAVE, WHICH CAN SAVE MEMORY BY PREVENTING THE CREATION OF A DYNAMIC __DICT__ FOR EACH INSTANCE.

- **HOW DO YOU IMPLEMENT A METHOD THAT ACTS LIKE A PROPERTY IN PYTHON?**

  - **EXPLANATION:** BY USING THE @PROPERTY DECORATOR, YOU CAN DEFINE A METHOD THAT ACTS AS A GETTER FOR A PRIVATE ATTRIBUTE.

- **WHAT IS THE PURPOSE OF @STATICMETHOD IN PYTHON?**

- **EXPLANATION:** @STATICMETHOD IS USED TO DEFINE A METHOD THAT DOES NOT DEPEND ON THE INSTANCE OF THE CLASS. IT CAN BE CALLED ON THE CLASS ITSELF RATHER THAN ON AN INSTANCE.

- **WHAT IS super() USED FOR IN PYTHON?**

  - **EXPLANATION:** super() IS USED TO CALL METHODS FROM A PARENT CLASS. IT IS TYPICALLY USED IN METHOD OVERRIDING TO CALL THE METHOD FROM THE SUPERCLASS.

- **CAN YOU MODIFY A PYTHON CLASS AT RUNTIME?**

  - **EXPLANATION:** YES, IN PYTHON, CLASSES ARE FIRST-CLASS OBJECTS, SO THEY CAN BE MODIFIED AT RUNTIME, ALLOWING FOR DYNAMIC BEHAVIOR.

- **WHAT ARE THE BENEFITS OF USING THE __REPR__ METHOD?**

  - **EXPLANATION:** THE __REPR__ METHOD PROVIDES A FORMAL STRING REPRESENTATION OF AN OBJECT, USEFUL FOR DEBUGGING AND LOGGING.

- **WHAT IS THE SIGNIFICANCE OF __INIT__ METHOD IN PYTHON?**

  - **EXPLANATION:** THE __INIT__ METHOD IS THE CONSTRUCTOR OF A CLASS. IT IS AUTOMATICALLY CALLED WHEN AN OBJECT IS INSTANTIATED AND IS USED TO INITIALIZE THE OBJECT'S ATTRIBUTES.

- **EXPLAIN THE DIFFERENCE BETWEEN SHALLOW COPY AND DEEP COPY IN PYTHON.**

  - **EXPLANATION:** A SHALLOW COPY CREATES A NEW OBJECT, BUT IT ONLY COPIES REFERENCES TO NESTED OBJECTS, NOT THE NESTED OBJECTS THEMSELVES. A DEEP COPY CREATES A COMPLETELY INDEPENDENT COPY, INCLUDING NESTED OBJECTS.

APPENDIX B: COMMON ERRORS AND DEBUGGING TIPS

IN PYTHON, DEBUGGING IS AN ESSENTIAL SKILL. HERE ARE SOME OF THE COMMON ERRORS PYTHON DEVELOPERS ENCOUNTER AND TIPS FOR DEBUGGING THEM.

- **WHAT IS AN INDENTATIONERROR IN PYTHON?**

  - **EXPLANATION:** AN INDENTATIONERROR OCCURS WHEN THERE IS AN ISSUE WITH THE INDENTATION IN PYTHON. PYTHON RELIES ON INDENTATION TO DEFINE CODE BLOCKS. MIXING SPACES AND TABS OR INCONSISTENT INDENTATION CAN TRIGGER THIS ERROR.
  - **TIP:** ALWAYS USE EITHER SPACES OR TABS FOR INDENTATION, AND CONFIGURE YOUR IDE TO HIGHLIGHT INDENTATION ISSUES.

- **WHAT IS A SYNTAXERROR IN PYTHON?**

  - **EXPLANATION:** A SYNTAXERROR OCCURS WHEN THE PYTHON INTERPRETER CANNOT PARSE THE CODE DUE TO INCORRECT SYNTAX, SUCH AS MISSING PARENTHESES OR AN EXTRA COLON.
  - **TIP:** CAREFULLY READ THE ERROR MESSAGE AND CHECK THE LINE WHERE THE ERROR OCCURRED. ENSURE PROPER SYNTAX, ESPECIALLY FOR PARENTHESES, COLONS, AND INDENTATION.

- **WHAT IS A NAMEERROR IN PYTHON?**

  - **EXPLANATION:** A NAMEERROR OCCURS WHEN YOU TRY TO USE A VARIABLE OR FUNCTION THAT HAS NOT BEEN DEFINED OR IS OUT OF SCOPE.
  - **TIP:** DOUBLE-CHECK THE SPELLING OF VARIABLES AND FUNCTIONS AND ENSURE THEY ARE PROPERLY DEFINED BEFORE USE.

- **WHAT IS A TYPEERROR IN PYTHON?**

  - **EXPLANATION:** A TYPEERROR OCCURS WHEN AN OPERATION OR FUNCTION IS APPLIED TO AN OBJECT OF AN INAPPROPRIATE TYPE, SUCH AS TRYING TO ADD A STRING TO AN INTEGER.
  - **TIP:** ENSURE THAT YOU ARE PERFORMING OPERATIONS ON COMPATIBLE DATA TYPES. USE THE TYPE() FUNCTION TO CHECK THE TYPES OF VARIABLES BEFORE PERFORMING OPERATIONS.

- **WHAT IS A VALUEERROR IN PYTHON?**

  - **EXPLANATION:** A VALUEERROR OCCURS WHEN A FUNCTION RECEIVES AN ARGUMENT OF THE CORRECT TYPE BUT AN INAPPROPRIATE VALUE, SUCH AS PASSING A NON-NUMERIC STRING TO INT().
  - **TIP:** ENSURE THAT VALUES PASSED TO FUNCTIONS OR METHODS ARE APPROPRIATE AND VALID FOR THE EXPECTED OPERATION. USE ERROR HANDLING WITH TRY-EXCEPT BLOCKS.

- **WHAT IS AN ATTRIBUTEERROR IN PYTHON?**

  - **EXPLANATION:** AN ATTRIBUTEERROR OCCURS WHEN AN INVALID ATTRIBUTE IS REFERENCED OR WHEN AN OBJECT DOES NOT HAVE THE ATTRIBUTE YOU ARE TRYING TO ACCESS.
  - **TIP:** CHECK THE OBJECT'S CLASS DEFINITION OR USE THE DIR() FUNCTION TO INSPECT ITS ATTRIBUTES AND METHODS.

- **WHAT IS A KEYERROR IN PYTHON?**

  - **EXPLANATION:** A KEYERROR OCCURS WHEN YOU TRY TO ACCESS A DICTIONARY KEY THAT DOES NOT EXIST.
  - **TIP:** BEFORE ACCESSING DICTIONARY KEYS, USE THE GET() METHOD OR CHECK IF THE KEY EXISTS WITH IF KEY IN DICT TO AVOID THIS ERROR.

- **WHAT IS AN INDEXERROR IN PYTHON?**

  - **EXPLANATION:** AN INDEXERROR OCCURS WHEN YOU TRY TO ACCESS AN INDEX THAT IS OUT OF RANGE FOR A SEQUENCE, LIKE A LIST OR STRING.
  - **TIP:** ALWAYS CHECK THE LENGTH OF SEQUENCES USING LEN() BEFORE TRYING TO ACCESS AN ELEMENT BY INDEX.

- **WHAT IS A ZERODIVISIONERROR IN PYTHON?**

  - **EXPLANATION:** A ZERODIVISIONERROR OCCURS WHEN YOU ATTEMPT TO DIVIDE A NUMBER BY ZERO.
  - **TIP:** USE CONDITIONAL STATEMENTS TO CHECK IF THE DENOMINATOR IS ZERO BEFORE PERFORMING DIVISION.

- **WHAT IS A FILENOTFOUNDERROR IN PYTHON?**

  - **EXPLANATION:** A FILENOTFOUNDERROR OCCURS WHEN TRYING TO OPEN OR READ A FILE THAT DOES NOT EXIST.
  - **TIP:** ENSURE THAT THE FILE PATH IS CORRECT. USE OS.PATH.EXISTS() TO CHECK IF THE FILE EXISTS BEFORE ATTEMPTING TO OPEN IT.

- **WHAT IS A MEMORYERROR IN PYTHON?**

  - **EXPLANATION:** A MEMORYERROR OCCURS WHEN THE PROGRAM RUNS OUT OF MEMORY WHILE ATTEMPTING TO ALLOCATE MORE SPACE.
  - **TIP:** OPTIMIZE MEMORY USAGE BY FREEING UP RESOURCES AND CHECKING FOR MEMORY LEAKS. CONSIDER USING GENERATORS TO HANDLE LARGE DATASETS.

- **WHAT IS A RECURSIONERROR IN PYTHON?**

  - **EXPLANATION:** A RECURSIONERROR OCCURS WHEN THE RECURSION DEPTH EXCEEDS THE MAXIMUM ALLOWED RECURSION LIMIT.
  - **TIP:** CHECK THE BASE CASE IN RECURSIVE FUNCTIONS TO ENSURE THAT RECURSION TERMINATES CORRECTLY. INCREASE THE RECURSION LIMIT USING SYS.SETRECURSIONLIMIT() IF NECESSARY.

- **WHAT IS AN IMPORTERROR IN PYTHON?**

  - **EXPLANATION:** AN IMPORTERROR OCCURS WHEN PYTHON CANNOT FIND THE MODULE OR PACKAGE YOU'RE TRYING TO IMPORT.
  - **TIP:** VERIFY THAT THE MODULE IS INSTALLED CORRECTLY USING PIP, AND CHECK THE PYTHON PATH OR ENVIRONMENT VARIABLES.

- **WHAT IS A TYPEERROR: 'NONETYPE' OBJECT IS NOT CALLABLE ERROR?**

  - **EXPLANATION:** THIS ERROR OCCURS WHEN YOU TRY TO CALL AN OBJECT THAT IS NONE.
  - **TIP:** ENSURE THAT FUNCTIONS OR METHODS ARE CORRECTLY DEFINED AND NOT MISTAKENLY ASSIGNED TO NONE.

- **WHAT IS A TYPEERROR: ARGUMENT OF TYPE 'X' IS NOT ITERABLE ERROR?**

  - **EXPLANATION:** THIS ERROR OCCURS WHEN YOU TRY TO ITERATE OVER AN OBJECT THAT IS NOT ITERABLE (E.G., AN INTEGER OR NONE).
  - **TIP:** CHECK IF THE OBJECT YOU ARE ITERATING OVER IS INDEED ITERABLE (E.G., A LIST, STRING, OR DICTIONARY).

- **WHAT IS A STOPITERATION ERROR IN PYTHON?**

  - **EXPLANATION:** A STOPITERATION ERROR IS RAISED WHEN A GENERATOR HAS NO MORE ITEMS TO YIELD.
  - **TIP:** ENSURE THAT YOUR LOOP OR ITERATOR CORRECTLY HANDLES THE END OF THE SEQUENCE BY USING A FOR LOOP OR HANDLING THE STOPITERATION EXCEPTION.

- **WHAT IS A NOTIMPLEMENTEDERROR IN PYTHON?**

  - **EXPLANATION:** A NOTIMPLEMENTEDERROR IS RAISED WHEN A METHOD OR OPERATION HAS NOT BEEN IMPLEMENTED YET, OFTEN IN ABSTRACT BASE CLASSES OR PLACEHOLDERS.
  - **TIP:** IMPLEMENT ALL NECESSARY METHODS IN YOUR CLASSES, OR RAISE THE EXCEPTION WITH A CLEAR MESSAGE INDICATING IT IS A PLACEHOLDER.

- **WHAT IS A CONNECTIONERROR IN PYTHON?**

  - **EXPLANATION:** A CONNECTIONERROR OCCURS WHEN A NETWORK CONNECTION FAILS.
  - **TIP:** ENSURE THAT THE NETWORK IS AVAILABLE AND HANDLE CONNECTION FAILURES WITH APPROPRIATE TRY-EXCEPT BLOCKS.

- **HOW CAN YOU DEBUG A TYPEERROR THAT OCCURS WITH A FUNCTION'S ARGUMENT?**

  - **EXPLANATION:** A TYPEERROR OCCURS WHEN THE ARGUMENT PASSED TO A FUNCTION IS OF THE WRONG TYPE. USE THE TYPE() FUNCTION TO CHECK THE ARGUMENT TYPES AND ENSURE THE FUNCTION PARAMETERS ARE RECEIVING THE CORRECT TYPES.

- **WHAT IS THE USE OF PDB IN PYTHON FOR DEBUGGING?**

  - **EXPLANATION:** PDB IS THE PYTHON DEBUGGER, A TOOL THAT ALLOWS YOU TO STEP THROUGH THE CODE, INSPECT VARIABLES, AND INTERACTIVELY DEBUG A PYTHON PROGRAM.
  - **TIP:** ADD IMPORT PDB; PDB.SET_TRACE() WHERE YOU WANT TO START DEBUGGING. USE COMMANDS LIKE N (NEXT), S (STEP INTO), C (CONTINUE), AND P (PRINT VARIABLE) TO INSPECT AND CONTROL EXECUTION.

- **HOW CAN YOU HANDLE MISSING OR INVALID INPUT DATA GRACEFULLY?**

  - **EXPLANATION:** YOU CAN HANDLE INVALID INPUT BY USING EXCEPTION HANDLING (TRY-EXCEPT) OR BY VALIDATING INPUT BEFORE PROCESSING.
  - **TIP:** USE TRY-EXCEPT BLOCKS TO CATCH INPUT-RELATED ERRORS, AND VALIDATE DATA WITH IF-ELSE STATEMENTS OR REGULAR EXPRESSIONS.

- **HOW CAN YOU HANDLE A KEYERROR WHEN ACCESSING A DICTIONARY?**

  - **EXPLANATION:** A KEYERROR OCCURS WHEN ACCESSING A DICTIONARY WITH A KEY THAT DOES NOT EXIST.
  - **TIP:** USE DICT.GET() TO PROVIDE A DEFAULT VALUE IF THE KEY DOES NOT EXIST, OR CHECK IF KEY IN DICT BEFORE ACCESSING THE KEY.

- **HOW CAN YOU RESOLVE AN ERROR CAUSED BY INCORRECT FILE PATHS?**

  - **EXPLANATION:** IF THE FILE PATH IS INCORRECT, A FILENOTFOUNDERROR WILL OCCUR.
  - **TIP:** CHECK THE FILE PATH FOR TYPOS, ENSURE THE FILE EXISTS, AND USE OS.PATH.EXISTS() TO VERIFY BEFORE ACCESSING FILES.

- **WHAT IS A COMMON CAUSE OF MEMORYERROR IN PYTHON?**

  - **EXPLANATION:** A MEMORYERROR OCCURS WHEN THE PROGRAM TRIES TO ALLOCATE TOO MUCH MEMORY.
  - **TIP:** TRY OPTIMIZING DATA STRUCTURES, USING GENERATORS, OR BREAKING LARGE TASKS INTO SMALLER CHUNKS TO REDUCE MEMORY USAGE.

  -

- **HOW CAN YOU DEBUG CODE WITH LOGIC ERRORS THAT DON'T THROW EXCEPTIONS?**

  - **EXPLANATION:** LOGIC ERRORS DO NOT RAISE EXCEPTIONS BUT PRODUCE INCORRECT RESULTS.
  - **TIP:** USE PRINT() STATEMENTS OR LOGGING TO TRACE VARIABLE VALUES AND PROGRAM FLOW. CONSIDER USING A DEBUGGER LIKE PDB FOR MORE ADVANCED INSPECTION.

1. **INDENTATIONERROR:**
   - ○ **EXPLANATION:** PYTHON USES INDENTATION TO DEFINE THE BLOCK OF CODE. AN INDENTATIONERROR OCCURS WHEN THE INDENTATION IS NOT CONSISTENT.
   - ○ **FIX:** ENSURE THAT THE CODE BLOCK IS INDENTED WITH SPACES OR TABS CONSISTENTLY. USE THE SAME NUMBER OF SPACES OR TABS THROUGHOUT THE FILE.

```
DEF FUNCTION():
    PRINT("THIS IS INDENTED CORRECTLY")
   PRINT("THIS WILL CAUSE AN INDENTATION ERROR")  # THIS LINE HAS INCORRECT INDENTATION
```

2. **TYPEERROR:**
   - ○ **EXPLANATION:** A TYPEERROR OCCURS WHEN AN OPERATION OR FUNCTION IS APPLIED TO AN OBJECT OF INAPPROPRIATE TYPE.
   - ○ **FIX:** CHECK THE TYPES OF OBJECTS YOU'RE WORKING WITH, AND ENSURE THAT OPERATIONS ARE COMPATIBLE WITH THOSE TYPES.

```
A = "STRING"
B = 10
RESULT = A + B  # TYPEERROR: CAN ONLY CONCATENATE STR (NOT "INT") TO STR
```

3. **NAMEERROR:**
   - ○ **EXPLANATION:** A NAMEERROR OCCURS WHEN A LOCAL OR GLOBAL NAME IS NOT FOUND. THIS HAPPENS WHEN YOU REFERENCE A VARIABLE OR FUNCTION THAT DOESN'T EXIST.
   - ○ **FIX:** ENSURE THAT THE VARIABLE OR FUNCTION IS DEFINED BEFORE IT IS USED.

```
PRINT(X)  # NAMEERROR: NAME 'X' IS NOT DEFINED
```

4. **ATTRIBUTEERROR:**
   - ○ **EXPLANATION:** AN ATTRIBUTEERROR OCCURS WHEN AN OBJECT DOES NOT HAVE THE SPECIFIED ATTRIBUTE OR METHOD.
   - ○ **FIX:** VERIFY THAT THE OBJECT HAS THE ATTRIBUTE OR METHOD BEING CALLED.

```
CLASS MYCLASS:
  DEF MY_METHOD(SELF):
    PASS

OBJ = MYCLASS()
OBJ.SOME_METHOD()  # ATTRIBUTEERROR: 'MYCLASS' OBJECT HAS NO ATTRIBUTE
'SOME_METHOD'
```

5. **INDEXERROR:**
   - ○ **EXPLANATION:** AN INDEXERROR OCCURS WHEN YOU TRY TO ACCESS AN ELEMENT FROM A LIST USING AN INDEX THAT IS OUT OF RANGE.
   - ○ **FIX:** ENSURE THAT THE INDEX YOU ARE ACCESSING IS WITHIN THE BOUNDS OF THE LIST.

```
MY_LIST = [1, 2, 3]
PRINT(MY_LIST[5])  # INDEXERROR: LIST INDEX OUT OF RANGE
```

6. **DEBUGGING TIPS:**
   - ○ **USE PRINT() STATEMENTS:** INSERT PRINT() STATEMENTS TO DISPLAY VARIABLE VALUES AND TRACK THE FLOW OF EXECUTION.
   - ○ **USE A DEBUGGER:** PYTHON'S BUILT-IN PDB DEBUGGER ALLOWS YOU TO STEP THROUGH YOUR CODE INTERACTIVELY, INSPECT VARIABLES, AND EVALUATE EXPRESSIONS.
   - ○ **CHECK STACK TRACE:** THE STACK TRACE WILL HELP YOU LOCATE THE SOURCE OF ERRORS, SHOWING YOU THE EXACT LINE AND TYPE OF ERROR.

7 KEYERROR:

EXPLANATION: A KEYERROR OCCURS WHEN YOU TRY TO ACCESS A DICTIONARY KEY THAT DOESN'T EXIST.

- **FIX:** USE DICT.GET() TO SAFELY ACCESS DICTIONARY KEYS OR CHECK IF THE KEY EXISTS USING IF KEY IN DICT.

```
MY_DICT = {"NAME": "ALICE"}
PRINT(MY_DICT["AGE"])  # KEYERROR: 'AGE'
```

8. VALUEERROR:

- **EXPLANATION:** A VALUEERROR IS RAISED WHEN A FUNCTION RECEIVES AN ARGUMENT OF THE CORRECT TYPE, BUT THE VALUE IS INAPPROPRIATE.
- **FIX:** ENSURE THAT FUNCTION ARGUMENTS ARE VALID. FOR EXAMPLE, PASS VALID NUMBERS TO INT() OR FLOAT().

```
NUM = INT("ABC")  # VALUEERROR: INVALID LITERAL FOR INT() WITH BASE 10: 'ABC'
```

9. IMPORTERROR:

- **EXPLANATION:** AN IMPORTERROR OCCURS WHEN PYTHON CANNOT LOCATE THE MODULE OR PACKAGE YOU ARE TRYING TO IMPORT.
- **FIX:** ENSURE THE MODULE IS INSTALLED OR THE PATH IS CORRECT.

```
IMPORT NONEXISTENT_MODULE  # IMPORTERROR: NO MODULE NAMED 'NONEXISTENT_MODULE'
```

10. FILENOTFOUNDERROR:

- **EXPLANATION:** A FILENOTFOUNDERROR IS RAISED WHEN ATTEMPTING TO OPEN A FILE THAT DOES NOT EXIST.
- **FIX:** VERIFY THE FILE PATH AND ENSURE THE FILE EXISTS BEFORE TRYING TO OPEN IT.

```
WITH OPEN("NONEXISTENT_FILE.TXT", "R") AS FILE:  # FILENOTFOUNDERROR: [ERRNO 2] NO SUCH FILE OR DIRECTORY
   CONTENT = FILE.READ()
```

11. TYPEERROR:

- **EXPLANATION:** A TYPEERROR OCCURS WHEN AN OPERATION OR FUNCTION IS APPLIED TO AN OBJECT OF INAPPROPRIATE TYPE.
- **FIX:** CHECK THE TYPES OF OBJECTS AND ENSURE THE OPERATION IS APPROPRIATE.

```
A = "HELLO"
B = 5
RESULT = A + B  # TYPEERROR: CAN ONLY CONCATENATE STR (NOT "INT") TO STR
```

12. RECURSIONERROR:

- **EXPLANATION:** A RECURSIONERROR OCCURS WHEN THE MAXIMUM RECURSION DEPTH IS EXCEEDED.
- **FIX:** ENSURE THAT YOUR RECURSIVE FUNCTION HAS A BASE CASE THAT STOPS FURTHER RECURSIVE CALLS.

```
DEF FACTORIAL(N):
    RETURN N * FACTORIAL(N-1) # RECURSIONERROR: MAXIMUM RECURSION DEPTH EXCEEDED
```

13. OVERFLOWERROR:

- **EXPLANATION:** AN OVERFLOWERROR OCCURS WHEN A NUMBER EXCEEDS THE RANGE OF A DATA TYPE, SUCH AS WHEN AN INTEGER IS TOO LARGE TO STORE IN MEMORY.
- **FIX:** CHECK FOR EXTREMELY LARGE NUMBERS AND CONSIDER USING DATA TYPES WITH HIGHER CAPACITY.

```
NUM = 1E1000 # OVERFLOWERROR: CANNOT CONVERT FLOAT INFINITY TO INTEGER
```

14. MEMORYERROR:

- **EXPLANATION:** A MEMORYERROR IS RAISED WHEN AN OPERATION RUNS OUT OF MEMORY, SUCH AS WHEN TRYING TO ALLOCATE TOO MUCH MEMORY FOR A LARGE DATASET.
- **FIX:** OPTIMIZE MEMORY USAGE, BREAK LARGE TASKS INTO SMALLER CHUNKS, OR USE GENERATORS INSTEAD OF LISTS.

```
LARGE_LIST = [0] * (10**10) # MEMORYERROR: CANNOT ALLOCATE MEMORY
```

15. MODULENOTFOUNDERROR:

- **EXPLANATION:** A MODULENOTFOUNDERROR OCCURS WHEN YOU TRY TO IMPORT A MODULE THAT DOESN'T EXIST OR ISN'T INSTALLED.
- **FIX:** ENSURE THAT THE MODULE IS INSTALLED USING PIP INSTALL AND VERIFY THE IMPORT STATEMENT.

```
IMPORT NONEXISTENT_MODULE # MODULENOTFOUNDERROR: NO MODULE NAMED 'NONEXISTENT_MODULE'
```

16. STOPITERATION:

- **EXPLANATION:** A STOPITERATION ERROR IS RAISED WHEN A GENERATOR OR ITERATOR HAS NO MORE ITEMS TO YIELD.
- **FIX:** USE A FOR LOOP INSTEAD OF MANUAL ITERATION, OR HANDLE THE STOPITERATION EXCEPTION.

```
MY_ITER = ITER([1, 2, 3])
PRINT(NEXT(MY_ITER))
PRINT(NEXT(MY_ITER))
PRINT(NEXT(MY_ITER))
PRINT(NEXT(MY_ITER))  # STOPITERATION
```

---

17. ASSERTIONERROR:

- **EXPLANATION:** AN ASSERTIONERROR OCCURS WHEN AN ASSERTION FAILS, MEANING THAT A CONDITION YOU EXPECTED TO BE TRUE IS FALSE.
- **FIX:** CHECK THE CONDITIONS THAT ARE BEING ASSERTED AND ENSURE THAT THE LOGIC IS CORRECT.

```
ASSERT 2 + 2 == 5  # ASSERTIONERROR: ASSERT 4 == 5
```

---

18. UNICODEDECODEERROR:

- **EXPLANATION:** A UNICODEDECODEERROR OCCURS WHEN PYTHON TRIES TO DECODE A FILE USING AN INCORRECT ENCODING.
- **FIX:** ENSURE THAT THE CORRECT ENCODING IS SPECIFIED WHEN READING A FILE.

```
WITH OPEN('FILE.TXT', 'R', ENCODING='UTF-8') AS FILE:
    CONTENT = FILE.READ()  # UNICODEDECODEERROR IF FILE IS NOT IN UTF-8
```

---

19. TIMEOUTERROR:

- **EXPLANATION:** A TIMEOUTERROR OCCURS WHEN A SYSTEM OPERATION EXCEEDS THE ALLOWABLE TIME LIMIT, SUCH AS WAITING FOR A RESPONSE FROM A NETWORK REQUEST.
- **FIX:** INCREASE THE TIMEOUT VALUE, OR HANDLE THE EXCEPTION BY RETRYING THE OPERATION.

```
IMPORT SOCKET
SOCKET.SETDEFAULTTIMEOUT(1)  # TIMEOUTERROR IF THE OPERATION TAKES TOO LONG
```

20. CONNECTIONERROR:

- **EXPLANATION:** A CONNECTIONERROR OCCURS WHEN A NETWORK CONNECTION IS UNSUCCESSFUL OR A NETWORK RESOURCE IS UNREACHABLE.
- **FIX:** CHECK THE NETWORK CONNECTION, HANDLE RETRIES, OR CHECK FOR A STABLE CONNECTION.

```
IMPORT REQUESTS
RESPONSE = REQUESTS.GET("HTTP://NONEXISTENTWEBSITE.COM")  # CONNECTIONERROR IF
WEBSITE IS UNREACHABLE
```

DEBUGGING TIPS FOR THESE ERRORS:

- **USE PRINT STATEMENTS:** INSERT PRINT() STATEMENTS TO TRACK VARIABLE VALUES AND PROGRAM FLOW.
- **USE DEBUGGING TOOLS:** UTILIZE PYTHON'S BUILT-IN PDB DEBUGGER TO STEP THROUGH YOUR CODE INTERACTIVELY.
- **CHECK STACK TRACES:** PAY ATTENTION TO THE ERROR MESSAGE AND STACK TRACE TO PINPOINT THE EXACT LINE WHERE THE ERROR OCCURRED.
- **HANDLE EXCEPTIONS GRACEFULLY:** USE TRY-EXCEPT BLOCKS TO CATCH AND HANDLE COMMON EXCEPTIONS WITHOUT CRASHING THE PROGRAM.

7.

APPENDIX C: ADDITIONAL RESOURCES FOR PYTHON LEARNERS

THIS SECTION INCLUDES RECOMMENDED RESOURCES FOR LEARNERS WHO WANT TO DIVE DEEPER INTO PYTHON.

1. **OFFICIAL PYTHON DOCUMENTATION:**
   - **LINK:** HTTPS://DOCS.PYTHON.ORG/
   - **EXPLANATION:** THE OFFICIAL PYTHON DOCUMENTATION IS THE BEST RESOURCE FOR UNDERSTANDING PYTHON'S BUILT-IN LIBRARIES, FUNCTIONS, AND FEATURES.

2. **PYTHON BOOKS:**
   - **"AUTOMATE THE BORING STUFF WITH PYTHON" BY AL SWEIGART:** A PRACTICAL GUIDE FOR BEGINNERS, TEACHING PYTHON THROUGH REAL-WORLD APPLICATIONS.
   - **"PYTHON CRASH COURSE" BY ERIC MATTHES:** AN EXCELLENT INTRODUCTION FOR BEGINNERS, COVERING BASIC PYTHON CONCEPTS AND BUILDING PROJECTS.
   - **"FLUENT PYTHON" BY LUCIANO RAMALHO:** A MORE ADVANCED BOOK FOR PYTHON DEVELOPERS LOOKING TO WRITE EFFICIENT AND IDIOMATIC PYTHON CODE.

3. **PYTHON ONLINE COURSES:**
   - **COURSERA (PYTHON FOR EVERYBODY):** A COMPREHENSIVE PYTHON COURSE BY DR. CHUCK (CHARLES SEVERANCE) THAT COVERS THE BASICS AND DATA STRUCTURES.
   - **UDEMY (COMPLETE PYTHON BOOTCAMP):** A POPULAR PYTHON COURSE ON UDEMY THAT COVERS PYTHON FROM SCRATCH, INCLUDING ADVANCED TOPICS.

4. **PYTHON COMMUNITY AND FORUMS:**
   - **STACK OVERFLOW:** GREAT FOR ASKING QUESTIONS AND FINDING SOLUTIONS TO COMMON PROGRAMMING PROBLEMS.
   - **REDDIT PYTHON:** THE PYTHON SUBREDDIT (R/LEARNPYTHON) IS A GREAT PLACE TO INTERACT WITH OTHER LEARNERS AND SHARE RESOURCES.

5. **PYTHON LIBRARIES AND FRAMEWORKS:**
   - **NUMPY:** FOR SCIENTIFIC COMPUTING AND NUMERICAL OPERATIONS.
   - **PANDAS:** FOR DATA MANIPULATION AND ANALYSIS.
   - **FLASK/DJANGO:** FOR BUILDING WEB APPLICATIONS.
   - **TENSORFLOW/PYTORCH:** FOR MACHINE LEARNING AND ARTIFICIAL INTELLIGENCE.

BY EXPLORING THESE RESOURCES, LEARNERS CAN ENHANCE THEIR PYTHON KNOWLEDGE AND KEEP UP WITH THE LATEST TRENDS IN PYTHON PROGRAMMING.

www.ingramcontent.com/pod-product-compliance
Lightning Source LLC
LaVergne TN
LVHW081755050326
832903LV00027B/1956